YELLOW DOGS, HUSH-PUPPIES, AND BLUETICK HOUNDS

YELLOW DOGS, HUSH-PUPPIES, AND BLUETICK HOUNDS

The Official *Encyclopedia of Southern Culture* Quiz Book

COMPILED BY LISA HOWORTH

with Jennifer Bryant

Published in collaboration with the

Center for the Study of Southern Culture

at the University of Mississippi by

The University of North Carolina Press

Chapel Hill & London

© 1996

The University of
North Carolina Press
All rights reserved
Design by Rich Hendel
Set in Cheltenham and Eagle
types by Keystone Typesetting, Inc.
Manufactured in the United States
of America
Library of Congress
Cataloging-in-Publication Data
Howorth, Lisa.
Yellow dogs, hushpuppies, and
bluetick hounds : the official
Encyclopedia of southern culture
quiz book / compiled by
Lisa Howorth.
p. cm.
ISBN 0-8078-4592-2
(pbk. : alk. paper)
1. Southern States – Miscellanea.
2. Southern States – Civilization –
Miscellanea. I. University of
Mississippi. Center for the Study of
Southern Culture. II. Encyclopedia
of southern culture. III. Title.
F209.H65   1996
975 – dc20   95-43523
CIP

00   99   98   97   96
5   4   3   2   1

DuBOIS

CONTENTS

FOREWORD

You may think that by putting myself forward in this way, I hope to leave the impression that I know the answers to all the questions in this book. Nothing could be further from the truth. Say that making an 80 on this book was one of the requirements (and not a bad idea at that) for being licensed to drive in the South. I like to *think* I could pass, but then again you might see me trudging alongside Highway 61 singing,

> Well I passed the pa'llel parkin',
> But that culchul quiz was cold,
> Lawd Lawd,
> Yes I passed the pa'llel parkin',
> But that culchul quiz was cold.
> Ain't seen no pa'llel parkin',
> Hushpuckena to Merigold.

What state would I be in, by the way?[1] and why?[2] Of course, if I had been the one to put together the questions in this book, myself, I probably could do all right on them. But although I do know *quite a bit* about southern culture, I can't be expected to know everything that Lisa Howorth and all the other people at the Center for the Study of Southern Culture know. Because that's their job. They're up studying southern culture every day from jus' kin to jus' cain't (which means what?[3]), busier than:

a) a one-legged clogger's foot
b) a Memphis lawyer on Judgment Day

---

1. Well hell, Mississippi. Where are you from, somewhere in France?
2. You got me there.
3. From when you just can see the sun in the morning, till when you just can't at night. You probably know that, unless you are from Europe somewhere, but I keep seeing it as "from cain't to cain't," which seems imprecise; and I always heard it "jus' kin to jus' cain't," and I wanted to take this opportunity to share that.

c) Daddy that time with the live alligator gar

d) all of the above.[4]

So you can be sure that this book is good wood turned in the grain. All too often the southern culture we see here and there is not the real scuppernong. I was reading in the *New York Times* just the other day where old John Egerton out of Nashville was saying, "With so much bogus barbecue, so much phony pie, Southern cookery is threatened to death by default." I know that's right. People sitting around eating that phony pie, not knowing enough to care. I tell you . . .

> Well Mama may have cussed the dog,
> And drank and run around,
> And sometimes cooked the pone too long,
> But pie-wise she was sound.
>
> She made it out of lard and grit
> And peaches and her love,
> And ev'rytime I think of it,
> I thank the stars above.
>
> Oh Heaven knows, and so do you,
> And Lord knows so do I,
> There's so much bogus barbecue
> And so much phony pie.
>
> But Daddy and us children knew
> That Mamma'd rather die
> Than to expose her loved ones to
> One bite of phony pie.

People are even practicing bogus voodoo! I venture to say so, although I did not grow up with voodoo myself. I grew up with Methodism. So I cannot speak from a lifetime of knowledge. But I have spent quite some time in New Orleans over the years, the vast majority of it at night, and when I read in the *New York Times* recently – this was a completely different article from the one on

4. d).

cooking – that there was some kind of nouveau voodoo going on in New Orleans, the hairs on the back of my neck stood up. And I saw that those hairs were on the money, when I read that the head priestess or "voodooienne," as the *Times* put it, "herself is white and came [to New Orleans] from Kennebunkport, Me."

Don't Kennebunkport *me*. I believe George Bush was from there. I'm not even going to bother going into voodoo economics, deep doo-doo, all that. I don't have to. This new voodoo thing is so trumped-up that even a New York paper can tell.

Many of the "devotees" of *arriviste* voodoo, according to the *Times*, "seem to be white people[5] – nose and tongue piercers, middle-aged intellectuals and men with foot-long pony tails – who enjoy the religion's drumming and cultural aspects."

There you go. They are in it for the cultural aspects. That is not how culture gets made. I am reminded of the Eudora Welty story (what's the title?[6]) in which concerned local folks are dragging the river for the body of a man's wife who has disappeared, and even the from-back-up-in-the-woods, bordering-on-feral Malones are helping with the net. But "the Malones," somebody says, "are just in it for the fish."[7]

Don't just be in this book for the cultural aspects, friends. Nor just for the fish. Be in it for the unknown. Until I read this book I don't believe I had ever heard of the Mad Potter of Biloxi or Rebecca Ann Latimer Felton, and I certainly never knew that okra could be used to increase the milk output of cows. Boiled or raw?[8] Raw, I'd imagine, just because I can't see who would take the time to fool with boiling up a big enough mess of okra to feed any significant number of cattle; but you'd think that if any kind of okra – if *anything* – would loosen up an udder, or anything else, it would be okra that had been boiled. Maybe udder-loosening isn't the point. Certainly no dairyperson would want an udder to get

5. Which means that for all intents and purposes they probably are.
6. "The Wide Net."
7. You'll be glad to learn that the man's wife turns out not to be in the river at all. The Malones get themselves an eel and an alligator and all kinds of things out of the deal.
8. I'd say raw. But I don't know.

too slick on the outside. One thing about this book: it leads, like the martin to its gourd (who used this figure of speech during the Watergate hearings?[9]), to further study.

I'll tell you something I was startled to learn. I was startled to learn that not only "gumbo," "tote," "goober," and so on come from Africa (I knew all that), but so do "unh-uh" and "uh-huh." It makes sense when you think about it, but then think about it again: This means that until well on into its decline maybe (when, exactly?[10]), European culture was oblivious to "unh-uh" and "uh-huh"? Think of the impact on a civilization that assumes it knows everything, for "unh-uh" and "uh-huh" to be revealed to it all of a sudden. (Too late, is liable to be the feeling of any southerner who has heard European rock and roll.)

A northern friend of mine was recently seated next to a southern woman at a benefit-for-the-arts banquet in some big city in Ohio or one of those states around in there. The southern woman was transplanted. She said she couldn't stand the North, because it "has no culture." My northern friend was nonplussed. There they were, after all, at a banquet for the benefit of the arts. The southern woman sensed his confusion.

"Oh I don't mean things like symphonies and operas," she said.

Good point. Symphonies and opera are *European* culture. All very well, but derivative of a civilization that got way ahead of itself before learning of "unh-uh" and "uh-huh."

You can see the effect of that premature sophistication in American lexicography today: I have not been able to find a single dictionary that bothers even to speculate on where "unh-uh" and "uh-huh" come from (although Webster's Third goes to the trouble of explaining that it is "a disyllabic sound with *m*-sounds at beginning and end, an *h*-like interval of voicelessness between, and heavier stress on the first member; in the registering of gratification the voiced members are more prolonged, about equal in stress, and the sound is higher in pitch"). And wait till you hear this: All those dictionaries leave out "unh-uh" entirely.

9. Senator Sam Ervin of North Carolina.
10. I don't know. Did Jelly Roll Morton tour there?

And claim to be unabridged!

In the bright lexicon of Webster (where was he from?[11]) there is no such word as "unh-uh." It's a good thing there are some books coming out of the South.

Roy Blount Jr.

11. New England somewhere.

PREFACE

Because it always seemed vastly more interesting to me to know that the body of the great explorer Hernando de Soto was chunked in the Mississippi River at approximately the same place where Jerry Lee Lewis was born (Ferriday, Louisiana; p. 51) and that four hundred and some years later, Mr. Lewis would reside in de Soto County, Mississippi (does the spirit of the great explorer live on in The Killer? Is there cosmic significance, or clues about finding gold, in "Great Balls of Fire"?) than to know what *Plessy v. Ferguson* was (p. 54), I wanted to call this little book *Head Full of Trash*. But my publisher was worried that the librarians and such, seeing the word "trash" in the title and fearing the worst, might not buy it. These publishing folks must be thinking of the sort of old-style, petticoat-insistent librarian that Eudora Welty describes in "A Sweet Devouring": "The librarian was the lady in town who wanted to be it. She called me by my full name and said, 'Does your mother know where you are? You know good and well the fixed rule of this library: *Nobody is going to come running back here with any book on the same day they took it out.* . . . And I can practically see through you!' " They *can't* be thinking of the razor-sharp librarians who supplied us with Robert Johnson's lyrics (p. 76) and found the number of manatees still in existence (p. 44) and hunted down the year Sarah Christian first competed in a NASCAR race (p. 41).

I admit it; my head is *hopelessly* full of trash, both schoolbook-variety and tabloidesque. But my position is, most anything important about any culture is going to be revealed in its trash. What do archeologists do all day, anyway? While I could never memorize things like Sidney Lanier's poem "Song of the Chattahoochee" (p. 24), I've always known the words to "Love in Vain" (p. 19), and it seems to me that the facts that a southern Miss America prayed over her leg and witnessed its two-inch growth (p. 11) and that the legendary Junior Johnson learned to drive stock cars by running moonshine in the North Carolina mountains (p. 38) reveal far more about southern culture than the date of the invention of the cotton gin (p. 28) or who the twelve Vanderbilt Agrarians were (p. 22). But publishers *do* have to worry; I suppose it's their job, and they do have reputations to uphold, not like some of us.

At any rate, the chosen title, admittedly neo-Grizzardian, does give the reader, or the trivialist, an idea about the breadth of this book. (Although why do so many titles about southernness always seem to boil down to either dogs, ignorance, or food made of corn?) Most, but not all, of these umpteen questions and answers are based on the *Encyclopedia of Southern Culture*, a big old thing (eight and a half pounds, to be exact) that has damn near everything in it that you could possibly want to know about the South. But I say *damn near*; it does not have everything. For instance, the *Encyclopedia* does not include information on grabbling (p. 41), or Ulysses S. Grant's feelings about the surrender at Appomattox (p. 54), or where the most cockroach-infested home is (p. 46), or who said "I'm sick and tired of being sick and tired" (p. 52), or who the Million Dollar Quartet was (p. 20). We think these extra questions are not only lagniappe (p. 10) but also help to illuminate the deep and abiding funkiness and humor and spirit of southern culture – that is to say, the things that made southerners and keep southerners as distinctive as they are.

How have we defined the South? Everyone does it differently. For instance, John Shelton Reed, the renowned, self-proclaimed Dixiologist, has suggested that the South might be "that part of the country where the people think they are all southerners." For this book, the South includes the eleven Confederate states, plus West Virginia, Kentucky, and Maryland when we felt like it because we were particularly fond of someone or particularly amazed by something.

We thought about making a scale – something like, if you answer 100 percent of the questions correctly, you *are* an Encyclopedia of Southern Culture; 80 percent, you have a real good idea about the difference between Shinola and that other stuff (p. 11); but only 15 percent, you get Shinola and the other stuff pretty confused, or "Yankee, go home." But why aggravate sectional differences? Being southern is a state of mind, not an IQ test, and with a guide like this, it might could be learned by anyone who is not, by the grace of God, actually *born* southern.

I'm sorry if we've left out someone's pet trivium, and about any mistakes. We intend this book to be entertaining and amusing but also informative. It's difficult to put it more eloquently than one of our student trivia grabbers did: "I don't like to think of it as trivia," he said, serious as a heart attack. "It's *knowledge*."

Many thanks to my friends who were able to tear themselves away from their various *haute* pursuits to assist me in my low ones: Ann and H. Dale Abadie, Pamela Arceneaux, Betty at the International Motor Sports Hall of Fame at Talladega, Jack Bass, Roy Blount, Mary Annie and Larry Brown, Jane Rule Burdine, Jimbob Cobb, Ed Croom, Nicky Bud Dawidoff, Michael Dean, William Duke (the Shelby Foote of North Sixteenth Street), Barbara Ewell and Jerry Speir, Bill Ferris, Bob Haws, Columbus Hopper, Richard and Vasser and Claire and M. H. Howorth, Anne Girline Jones, Christy Keirn, Edward Komara, Susan and Tim Lee, Andy McKay, John Hawkins Napier III, the reference department of the J. D. Williams Library at the University of Mississippi, Sparky, David Sansing, Wendy Shay, Aleda Shirley, Brenda and Bill West, Rod Williams, and Charles Reagan Wilson. Thanks also to David Perry, Christi Stanforth, and others at the University of North Carolina Press, and to our resourceful graduate students, whose heads are endless repositories of southern-culture-related trash: Susan Glisson, Elizabeth Hargood, Pat Hodo, Jay Langdale, Patrick McIntyre, Ron Nurnberg, Elvis Renberg, Bland Whitley, Chuck Yarborough, and especially Marty Gould, who, in spite of bad cases of San Joaquin Valley Fever and culture shock, was busier with trivia than a one-legged man in an ass-kicking contest.

Lisa Howorth

QUESTIONS

MANNERS, MYTH, AND RELIGION

The South . . . has been a kind of Sphinx on the American land.
– David Potter, The South and the Sectional Conflict

1 What, according to William Faulkner, would "work for you ten years for the chance to kick you once"?

2 Paul Prudhomme put what New Orleans Cajun restaurant on the map and what scorched fish on the menu?

3 What is gullah?

4 In his 1980 book, *Crackers*, Roy Blount suggests that this southern appellation means pretty much the same as "mensch." What is it?

5 By what name are green peas known in the South?

6 On the morning of May 23, 1934, six law officers fired more than 160 shots at a car driving down a road near Arcadia, Louisiana. Who died in that hail of bullets?

7 What is filé?

8 What private, exclusive subscription ball, still held annually in Charleston, began in 1762 as a musical society?

9 According to a study by John Shelton Reed, southerners are significantly more likely than non-southerners to say they believe in which of the following: God, the Devil, voodoo, or ghosts?

10 What is an A.M.E. church?

11 Where is the biannual crawfish festival held?

12 What are the likely roots of the derogatory term "cracker," as in "Georgia cracker"?

13 What is a "haint" or a "hant"?

14 Where is the Chittlin' Strut Festival?

15 Who founded the Moral Majority?

16 The New Year's Eve Ball in Montgomery, the Camellia Ball in Mobile, the Bal du Bois in Richmond, the Halloween Ball in Atlanta, the Beaux Arts Ball in Birmingham, and the Terpsichorean Ball in Dallas are all examples of what?

17 What is the most commonly consumed hard liquor in the South?

18 Who is the subject of this African American recitation – the old Tarbaby, the bad alligator, the nasty old possum, or the signifying monkey?

> Down in the jungle near a dried-up creek
> The _____ hadn't slept for a week
> Remembering the ass-kicking he had got in the past
> He had to find somebody to kick the lion's ass.

19 True or false?: *Southern Living* magazine was founded by the publishers of *Time*, *Life*, and other national magazines.

20 Where is the National Storytelling Festival held?

21 Where was the world's biggest mule market?

22 What is the most famous southern Appalachian vendetta?

23 What was the first fraternity to be founded and take permanent root in the South?

24 What was the first Greek-letter women's social organization in the United States?

25 What is the name for the theory that man and earth were created in an instant by the Supreme Being?

26 What young Virginia woman served as a missionary to China and became the inspiration for extensive fund-raising by Southern Baptist women?

27 What is "pot likker": the kid who hangs around to clean the pan during cake making, the juice left over from the cooking of greens, or a lawman who hunts out marijuana patches?

28 What day of the week is still a half-day holiday in many small southern towns?

29 What is a bluetick hound?

30 What southern institution served as a dispensary for medicine, gossip, news, weather reports, credit, commodities, farm and personal advice, and political opinion?

31 From 1897 to 1917, New Orleans had a legally established district for prostitution. What was it called?

32 What is the "City Too Busy to Hate"?

33 What percent of southerners own guns: 65 percent, 80 percent, or 90 percent?

34 Grits, hominy, dogbread, hoecake, mush, fritters, spoonbread, hushpuppies, and johnny cake are all made with what?

35 What must southerners always eat on New Year's Day to insure good luck all year?

36 In the rest of the world, it's cowpeas and rice. In South Carolina, it's what?

37 Traditionally, whiskey, Peychaud bitters, and sugar, served in an Old-Fashioned glass rinsed with absinthe. What is the name of this peculiarly New Orleans drink?

38 Where do southern Presbyterians traditionally summer?

39 According to a famous University of Alabama fraternity toast, what was "pure and chaste as this sparkling water, as cold as this gleaming ice"?

40 What popular holiday was originally celebrated by black Texans to commemorate emancipation?

41 What southern Pentecostal group remains predominantly black and maintains its headquarters in Memphis?

42 What is a feist?

43 The words "boogie," "gumbo," "tote," "goober," "cooter," "okra," "jazz," "hoodoo," and "uh-huh" and "unh-uh" originated where?

44 What product was advertised throughout the South on ubiquitous sets of sequential signs?

45 To enhance the flavor of a cola drink, what will southerners sometimes add to the bottle?

46 When does Mardi Gras take place?

47 Who founded the first Catholic newspaper in the United States and opened the first Roman Catholic seminary in the South?

48 What ethnic Protestant sect founded the North Carolina towns of Bethabara, Bethania, and Salem between 1753 and 1766?

49 What is the "Arkansas Traveler"?

50 The South had two Shaker settlements. Where were they?

51 Who were the "lubbers"?

52 What town is said by some to produce the nation's best country ham?

53 What social fraternity celebrates its southern heritage with Old South Week?

54 What South Carolina theme park was hailed, in its heyday, as a "spiritual Disneyland"?

55 Who was a "steel-driving man"?

56 What is glossolalia?

57 What are *fais-do-dos*?

58 The greatest number of "churched" southerners belong to one of two Protestant denominations. What are they?

59 The fifty-five-foot-high, cast-iron statue of Vulcan, the Roman god of fire and metalworking, looks down on what city?

60 What is "scrape"?

61 What is a "linthead"?

62 What prestigious university memorialized her 136 sons who died to preserve the Union but to this day has never acknowledged her 64 sons who died for the Confederacy?

63 The Seminole Indians are a subtribe of what?

64 How did the people of North Carolina come to be called "Tar Heels"?

65 Where was the first Sunday school in the South?

66 Tarpon Springs, Florida, has a large and important population of what ethnic group?

67 The strong Scottish influence in the South is celebrated where?

68 In New Orleans's Mardi Gras celebrations, Comus, Momus, Proteus, and Rex are some of the participating social clubs. What is the name for these groups?

69 What snack was traditionally consumed with an RC Cola: a Moon Pie, a York Patty, a Slim Jim, or pork rinds?

70 What is a roux?

71 What traditionally all-male college gives its entering freshmen a booklet entitled "To Manner Born, to Manner Bred: A Hip Pocket Guide to Etiquette"?

72 What do squash, corn, beans, and sweet potatoes have in common?

73 What Trappist monk, author of the spiritual autobiography *The Seven Storey Mountain* (1948), lived in the Cistercian monastery in Gethsemani, Kentucky?

74 What southern town has the smallest Jewish synagogue in the United States and raises the world's sweetest onions?

75 What is a "mojo hand" or "mojo"?

76 What is a Treeing Walker?

77 Who were the first ethnic Protestants to come to the South?

78 In the 1960s, two of the most recognizable faces on earth belonged to Kentuckians. Who were they?

79 What popular member of the gourd family, an annual called *citrullus lanatus*, is still known to some southerners as "Depression ham"?

80 What is the most successful of the southern Junior League cookbooks?

81 What is New Orleans's most popular beer?

82 As measured by per capita income, what are this country's two poorest states?

83 What bread usually accompanies a fried-fish meal?

84 What is spoonbread?

85 Where is the annual Spoleto Festival held?

86 Who was the "Texas Tornado," a pastor regarded by many as the father of modern fundamentalism?

87 What are redbones?

88 From the following list, select the only non-southern televangelist whose electronic church is neither broadcast from the South nor concerned with a southern audience: Robert Schuller, Billy Graham, Rex Humbard, Jerry Falwell, Pat Robertson, Jimmy Swaggart, Richard De Hann, or D. James Kennedy.

89 Where is the National Civil Rights Museum located?

90 When was the popular Ford F-series pickup truck introduced?

91 What organization was created in 1894 by women who saw themselves as guardians of the Lost Cause?

92 Who once said, "Southerners will vote dry as long as they can stagger to the polls"?

93 Where is the Museum of the Southern Jewish Experience located?

94 What stereotypical family member, a favorite character of southern fiction, was often influential and indispensable within the family circle but was denied the status that southern society accorded to matrons and mothers?

95 Who was born on a mountaintop in Tennessee?

96 What does the traditional holiday dish called ambrosia contain?

97 What treat is, according to the Standard Candy Company, a southern baby's first request?

98 What mother and daughter of the same name were widely celebrated voodoo priestesses during a fifty-year period in the middle of the nineteenth century?

99 How do natives of New Orleans pronounce the local street names Chartres, Burgundy, Carondelet, and Freret?

100 What French hero of the American Revolution loved grits so much that he took a substantial supply back to France?

101 What liquor comes in a "square shooter" bottle?

102 What is the Cajun Christmas custom called *feux de joie*?

103 What specific biblical passage is cited by some Appalachian Pentecostal groups as the inspiration to "take up serpents"?

104 What Mississippian was food editor of the *New York Times* for thirty-one years?

105 What southern states still observe Confederate Memorial Day?

106 What does the word "tump" mean?

107 Delicious jellies and wine can be made from what two native grapes?

108 What does "F.F.V." stand for?

109 What is a southerner most likely to be "hit upside of"?

110 In what New Orleans restaurant were oysters Rockefeller first served?

111 What old New Orleans restaurant does not take reservations, requires male diners to wear ties, and is a favorite lunch spot of New Orleans families?

112 What South Carolina town is the birthplace of W. J. Cash and home to the Peachoid?

113 Where is the original Doe's Eat Place?

114 What is a "yat"?

115 What are chitterlings, or chitlins?

116 What was the "Saratoga of the South"?

117 What headache preparations is a rural southerner most likely to take?

118 What drink is emblematic of the South but is now rarely consumed there, except on Kentucky Derby Day?

119 What first-born son of fundamentalist Presbyterians from Charlotte, North Carolina, has preached to more people than any other Christian in the world?

120 In 1840, Baptists and Methodists attempted to burn this southern university because they thought the Anglicans and Presbyterians on the school's Board of Regents were discriminating against them. Which school was it?

121 Between 1921 and 1929, five states passed laws prohibiting the teaching of evolution. Name three of them.

122 What is believed to be the only restaurant in the world in which grilled peanut butter and banana sandwiches (a favorite of Elvis Presley) are found on the menu?

123 What Deep South snack was associated with cotton-picking and -ginning season and now is most often seen at roadside stands?

124 Who are the Cajuns?

125 What religious cult entered America in the latter part of the eighteenth century, when the French brought slaves from Haiti to Louisiana?

126 What is the difference between sour mash and bourbon?

127 In the eastern Carolinas, what ingredients does barbecue sauce traditionally contain?

128 Where is the Junior Miss Pageant held?

129 "Eat _____ and love longer."

130 Beauty pageants get a lot of attention in the South – and a lot of support from participants and sponsors. Some twenty states have never had a Miss America; however, only one of those is in the Confederate South. Which state is it?

131 Where are sesame seeds referred to as "benne seeds"?

132 What tribe of native Americans is the largest tribe east of the Mississippi and also the largest federally unrecognized tribe in the United States?

133 In Louisiana, what saucy meat dish is commonly served with grits?

134 What is the origin of the word "tacky"?

135 How many Miss Americas have attended the University of Mississippi?

136 Where is the Saturn Bar?

137 Where does the Southern cross the Yellow Dog?

138 What young North Carolinian published *Southern Cooking*, which combined the best traditional southern recipes with extensive knowledge of food and technique?

139 What caramelized nut and sugar confection appeared in Louisiana as early as 1762?

140 What are the ingredients for Brunswick stew?

141 What university was founded by Baptist minister Pat Robertson?

142 What is a catahoula hog dog?

143 What is a jenny, and what is a henny?

144 America's most successful utopian community began in 1914 in California but for twenty-five years thrived in Louisiana, where 10,000 people came to call the colony home. What was its name?

145 What social fraternity counts Emmitt Smith, Jerry Rice, Karl Malone, and George Washington Carver among its members?

146 What does the word "lagniappe" mean?

147 What is the motto of evangelist Rick Stanley, stepbrother of Elvis Presley?

148 What heterosexual Nashville Republican was a public cross-dresser known for his particularly shapely legs?

149 What does "teeninecy" mean?

150 Who was folk hero Henry Berry Lowrie?

151 What are *andouille* and *tasso*?

152 What man from Chesapeake, Virginia, head of the Christian Coalition, has been called "the right hand of God" by *Time* magazine?

153 What are Old Sparky and Yellow Mama?

154 Who is the most famous former resident of Ashland, Kentucky?

155 What are melungeons?

156 What southern first lady has a village of "untouchables" in Bangladesh named for her?

157 What religious organization, formed in 1845 by men who defended slavery as biblical, has formally apologized to African Americans and denounced slavery and racism as sins against the Lord?

158 What was Dixie Peach?

159 Alabama ranks second in the nation in the number of what legally sanctioned punishments?

160 What are pork fries?

161 What church recently raised $2,500 for a new sanctuary with its nighttime "Coon Hunt for Christ"?

162 How is the honorific "Mrs." sometimes pronounced in the rural Deep South?

163 When you bisect something, you cut it _____.

164 Where are the following museums located?: the National Museum of the Boy Scouts of America; the Country Doctor Museum; the Warren Rifles Confederate Museum; the Patent Model Museum; the Schmidt Museum of Coca-Cola Memorabilia; and the Museum of Tobacco Art and History.

165 What does the expression "brokedick" mean?

166 The world's largest voluntary organization for girls was founded in this southern city. What are the names of the organization and the town?

167 Which Miss America claimed that her leg, injured in an accident, spontaeously sprouted an extra two inches in length?

168 Complete this sentence: "He don't know shit from _____."

169 Where is the Pony Penning held every July?

170 What entrepreneur from Lexington, Kentucky, would try to entice one to buy a silk dress from his catalog by describing it this way: "You wore it to that party in the Village where you met William Faulkner and Robert Lowell. Faulkner was gracious, courtly. Lowell burned with intensity. It made you weak in the knees." He further describes the dress as having polka dots "the size of small garbanzos; lemur eyes; hummingbird hearts."

171 What does the word "cooter" mean?

172 In 1984, at a festival in Ayden, North Carolina, C. Mort Horst set a world record by eating seven and a half pounds of this vegetable in thirty minutes. What was the vegetable?

173 According to Florence King, the South contains the phenomenon of the "self-rejuvenating virgin," who, among other deceptions, relied on that "most southern of all contraceptives." What is it?

174 Name at least three typical roadside messages of salvation.

175 What plant, when eaten, can either delight or kill you, depending on which part you eat?

176 Natives of which region of the South pronounce "aunt" with a broad "a," "can't" with the vowel of "paint," and "house" as "hoose"?

MUSIC AND ENTERTAINMENT

*The colored folk been singin' it and playin' it just the way
I'm doin' now, man, for more years than I know. Nobody paid it
no mind 'til I goosed it up. – Elvis Presley*

1 True or false?: Actress Vivien Leigh, who created the roles of the fiery southern belle Scarlett in *Gone with the Wind* and the tragic Blanche DuBois in *A Streetcar Named Desire*, was British.

2 Match the stars with their roles and movies in these Tennessee Williams adaptations:

Katharine Hepburn	Stanley Kowalski	*Baby Doll*
Carroll Baker	Brick	*Sweet Bird of Youth*
Marlon Brando	Violet Venable	*Suddenly Last Summer*
Paul Newman	Tom	*Glass Menagerie*
Natalie Wood	Baby Doll	*Cat on a Hot Tin Roof*
Kirk Douglas	Alva	*A Streetcar Named Desire*
Ed Begley	Boss Finley	*This Property Is Condemned*

3 Whose husband was driven out of their coalfield town by company police, inspiring her to write the classic labor song "Which Side Are You On"?

4 What "Blue Yodeler" is known as the "Father of Country Music"?

5 Match these three Mississippi musicians with their stage names:

McKinley Morganfield (1915–1983)	Howlin' Wolf
Chester Burnett (1910–1976)	Bo Diddley
Ellas McDaniel (b. 1928)	Muddy Waters

6 Of these plays by southerners that attempt to portray the African American condition, which one was written by an African American: *When the Jack Hollers*, *Porgy and Bess*, or *In Abraham's Bosom*?

7 Pogo Possum, Albert Alligator, and Porky Porcupine are fictional denizens of what southern wilderness?

8 What was the stage name of Bill Robinson, a popular African American tap dancer from Richmond and Louisville?

9 Who was Satchmo?

10 What song and dance was the trademark of Memphian Rufus Thomas, who began his musical career on the minstrel circuit?

11 Whose guitar is named "Lucille"?

12 What was the title of D. W. Griffith's 1915 film, which depicted blacks as evil and a threat to the southern way of life?

13 What is another name for Sacred Harp singing, which flourished in churches in the late eighteenth and early nineteenth centuries and is still practiced in rural churches in the Deep South?

14 Name at least three blind blues musicians.

15 Whose Kentucky band developed an innovative ensemble-band style based on the vocal and instrumental styles of early fiddle bands?

16 Who wrote and performed the theme song for the 1960s TV show *The Beverly Hillbillies*?

17 Who "didn't know nothin' 'bout birthin' no babies"?

18 What group of Mardi Gras Indians recorded a collaborative album with members of the Meters, the Neville Brothers, and Big Chief Jolley?

19 What dance was named the state dance by the South Carolina legislature in 1985?

20 What fiddler was the first living musician to be elected to the Country Music Hall of Fame?

21 Who wrote and sang this 1930s protest song?:

> I was raised in old Kentucky
>
> In Kentucky borned and bred,
>
> And when I joined the union
>
> They called me a Russian Red.

22 What rockabilly musician, known as "The Killer," is the cousin of televangelist Jimmy Swaggart and country musician/entrepreneur Mickey Gilley?

23 Who "ran through the briars and they ran through the brambles. Ran through the bushes where the rabbits couldn't go. Ran so fast the hounds couldn't catch 'em. On down the Mississippi to the Gulf of Mexico"?

24 What Memphis radio station was the first station in the South to adopt an all-black format?

25 What two comic strip characters, both introduced in 1934, encouraged Americans to think of southern mountain folk as backward, lazy, and dumb?

26 What southern mountain lap instrument allows the player to produce a soft and slightly melancholy sound by playing the melody on the nearest string while letting the other strings drone?

27 In 1932, this radio station, operating with excessive wattage from across the Mexican border near Del Rio, Texas, gave airplay to and popularized much southern country and gospel music. What were its call letters?

28 In what states were Walton's Mountain and Mayberry set?

29 What form of southern mountain dance probably evolved out of the folk dances of Scotch, Irish, and English immigrants but was also influenced by traveling black minstrels and Native American ceremonial dances?

30 Who has been called "the Mouth of the South"?

31 What civil rights movement song, adapted from an old black hymn, was the official theme song of the 1963 March on Washington?

32 In what 1964 film did Bette Davis play a southern belle cleared of thirty-seven years of guilt for a murder she did not commit?

33 What TV cousins had a souped-up Dodge Charger named "General Lee"?

34 Who walked tall (6'6", to be exact) in McNairy County, Tennessee?

35 From what 1972 film is the immortal line "Squeal like a pig" taken?

36 Who jumped off the Tallahatchie Bridge?

37 What Georgia-born soul singer hung out on the dock of the bay watching the tide roll away?

38 True or false?: Johnny Cash sings with such authority about prison life in such songs as "Folsom Prison Blues" and "I Walk the Line" because he is a convicted felon who has spent considerable time in jail.

39 What building housed the Grand Ole Opry for thirty-one years?

40 What Elvis film, set in New Orleans, was an adaptation of the Harold Robbins novel *A Stone for Danny Fisher*?

41 What resident of greater Augusta, Georgia, is the Godfather of Soul?

42 Among the many songs of the "Father of Gospel," Thomas A. Dorsey, is one that has been translated into thirty-two languages, recorded by the fourteen-year-old Aretha Franklin, and sung by Mahalia Jackson at the funeral of Martin Luther King Jr. What is it?

43 Virginia Patterson Hensley of Winchester, Virginia, grew up to be a popular country-and-western singer. What was her stage name?

44 In what dance, originally from Appalachia, do groups of four male-female couples dance to fiddle music and the chanted instructions of a caller?

45 What popular gospel quartet from Ackerman, Mississippi, has recorded over one hundred albums and many more singles since the 1940s?

46 "Chanky-chank" describes what kind of music?

47 What folk hero railroad engineer is immortalized in songs by Mississippi John Hurt, the Grateful Dead, and the Boy Scout songbook?

48 Ferdinand Le Menthe is the real name of what legendary New Orleans jazz pianist?

49 By blending the European romantic tradition with black rhythms and Creole melodies, this musician became one of the most renowned American classical composers of the mid-nineteenth century. Who was he?

50 What popular contemporary comic strip set in Bypass, North Carolina, satirizes the culture and mystique of the South?

51 What actress played Mammy in *Gone with the Wind*?

52 What 1978 film championed the struggle of North Carolina textile workers?

53 What recording studio was established in 1969 in Macon, Georgia, by the late Otis Redding's manager?

54 Match these country-music performers with their native states:

Willie Nelson	North Carolina
Patsy Cline	Mississippi
Roy Acuff	Texas
Bill Monroe	Tennessee
Charley Pride	Virginia
Earl Scruggs	Kentucky

55 What Alabama native inspired Tennessee Williams's Blanche DuBois, was an emcee on radio's "Big Show" in the 1950s, and shares her name with a small town in northern Louisiana?

56 What famous opera star from Laurel, Mississippi, starred in Broadway's *Porgy and Bess* from 1952 to 1954, and in 1955 made her professional grand opera debut in *Tosca*?

57 What is America's longest-running radio program?

58 What famous country singer made his debut at age fourteen singing "WPA Blues" in an Alabama talent show?

59 Who was the first woman in country music to have her own syndicated television show?

60 What former Miss America starred with Elvis in *Girl Happy* and *Harum Scarum*?

61 What TV show, centered around family members Amos, Luke, Kate, Little Luke, and Hassie, was the first sitcom to feature southerners?

62 Match these southern-born jazz musicians with their instruments:

Lester Young	Trumpet
King Oliver	Tenor saxophone
Jelly Roll Morton	Clarinet
Pete Fountain	Cornet
Louis Armstrong	Piano

63 Who is the "Father of the Blues"?

64 What song popularized by Billie Holiday lamented lynchings?

65 What popular hymn was written by an Englishman who served as first mate on a slave ship?

66 What southern anthem was probably written by an Ohioan, Daniel Emmett, just before the outbreak of the Civil War?

67 What Hollywood star, a native of Waycross, Georgia, became the first real male nude centerfold when he appeared in *Cosmopolitan* magazine in 1972?

68 What old spiritual illustrates the slaves' identification with the Old Testament plight of the Jews in Egypt?

69 What Mississippi highway was, according to a song by Bob Dylan (b. 1941), "where all that killin' got done"?

70 What musical composition by Aaron Copland captures the beauty and mystery of the southern mountains?

71 What is "Parchman Farm," immortalized in a blues song written by Booker White (1906–77) and recorded by Mose Allison?

72 What was on bluesman Robert Johnson's trail?

73 Who had friends named Weyman C. Wanamaker, Curtis "Fruit Jar" Hainey, and Kathy Sue Loudermilk?

74 What southeastern mountains are the subject of a late-nineteenth-century folksong, in which they are "covered with snow"?

75 What north/south train was made famous in a song written by Steve Goodman and recorded by Arlo Guthrie?

76 What type of Creole dance music relies on Acadian or Afro-American blues tunes, highly syncopated Afro-Caribbean rhythms, the vest *frottoir*, and the German accordion?

77 What New Orleans R&B singer made a hit in 1966 with the song "Tell It Like It Is" and now sings about the fabric of our lives?

78 Who wrote the inspirational gospel song "I'll Fly Away"?

79 What gonzo journalist, the model for Uncle Duke in the comic strip "Doonesbury," hails from Louisville, Kentucky?

80 Where did the banjo originate?

81 What pop singer, born in Mobile, Alabama, in 1946, likes his cheeseburger with "lettuce and tomato, Heinz 57 and french-fried potatoes"?

82 What Alice Walker novel was made into a movie in 1985?

83 What type of animal was Misty, and where did she live?

84 Born in Boston, Massachusetts, in 1948, but raised in Chapel Hill, North Carolina, this pop singer is often associated with the South because of songs like "Carolina in My Mind," "Copperline," "Shed a Little Light," and "Country Road."

85 Match these southern rock bands with the locales that gave them their start:

Allman Brothers	Jacksonville, Fla.
Marshall Tucker Band	Nashville
Lynyrd Skynyrd	Memphis
Charlie Daniels Band	Spartanburg, S.C.
Amazing Rhythm Aces	Macon, Ga.

86 What variety show, first aired in 1969, featured first-rate country music and some of the world's corniest one-liners?

87 What 1977 movie featured a high-speed beer run from Texas to Georgia, car crashes, CB jabber, an "escaped" bride, and a stereotypical good old boy sheriff?

88 What rock and roll singer, born in Macon, Georgia, in 1933, played a transvestite named Lavonne in gay clubs early in his career?

89 What was the flip side of Elvis Presley's first hit, "That's All Right, Mama"?

90 Lynyrd Skynyrd's epic fourteen-minute live recording of "Free Bird" was made in what historic Atlanta venue?

91 What two Robert Johnson songs were popularized by the Rolling Stones and Cream?

92 Who "fell down in a burnin' ring o' fire"?

93 What albino blues musician is a native of Beaumont, Texas?

94 What Hollywood film star bought a Georgia town?

95 What 1980s CBS television show, set in Atlanta, originally starred Delta Burke, Dixie Carter, Jean Smart, Annie Potts, and Meshach Taylor?

96 In the 1920s, this "Empress of the Blues" rose to the pinnacle of her profession and became the highest-paid black entertainer of her day.

97 In the movie *Greased Lightning*, Richard Pryor portrayed the only African American to have competed regularly on the NASCAR circuit. Who was the driver?

98 What is the tackiest hotel and entertainment complex in the United States and possibly in the world?

99 Who is the "King of Zydeco"?

100 This is the first verse of what song?:

I was standin' by the window
On one cold and cloudy day
When I saw the hearse come rolling
For to carry my mother away.

101 What Georgia town is associated with the B-52's, R.E.M., and Widespread Panic?

102 What Alabama town was famous for its recording studios, where the Rolling Stones, Aretha Franklin, Otis Redding, Joe Tex, Percy Sledge, and Wilson Pickett, among others, laid down tracks?

103 What perky NBC newscaster is a native Virginian with family roots in Alabama?

104 Name three southern musicians who died in plane crashes.

105 What Memphis cult musician first gained fame with his recording of "The Letter" (1967) and then had a band called Big Star?

106 What was the name of the fictitious shrimp company founded by Forrest Gump?

107 What was the title of Robert Altman's 1975 film about Music City, USA?

108 Who was the large-thumbed Richmond heroine of Tom Robbins's *Even Cowgirls Get the Blues* (1976)?

109 Who is Bocephus?

110 What two rock stars from Macon, Georgia, members of the same legendary band, were killed in separate motorcycle accidents within only three blocks and one year of each other?

111 What was the "Million Dollar Quartet"?

112 According to a number 1 hit by Lloyd Price, who shot Billy?

113 Who rocked around the Christmas tree?

114 What number-one hit by Ray Charles is now the official state song of Georgia?

115 Who was the worst person New Orleans singer Ernie K-Doe knew?

116 To what event did Louis Armstrong attribute his starting a musical career?

117 What quartet from Staunton, Virginia, was discovered by

Johnny Cash in 1964, the year before their big crossover hit "Flowers on the Wall"?

118 Of these southern-born blues performers, which one is not from the Mississippi Delta: W. C. Handy, John Lee Hooker, B. B. King, or Muddy Waters?

119 What rock and roll disc jockey, whose gravelly voice was broadcast across the entire United States in the early 1960s, died recently at his home in Belvidere, North Carolina?

120 In 1954, Elvis Presley made one of his only two TV commercials. What was he advertising: Cadillacs, Wild Root Hair Creme, Humko Cooking Oil, or Southern Made Doughnuts?

121 A character played by this native Chattanoogan preached from Ezekiel 25 in the hit movie *Pulp Fiction*.

122 A band from Chapel Hill, North Carolina, takes its name from which of the following candies: Mary Janes, Rock 'n' Roll Stage Planks, Squirrel Nut Zippers, or Pure King Leo?

123 In October 1963, children in Washington, D.C., were entertained by a man wearing a hat shaped like a tray holding a burger, fries, and milkshake; shoes shaped like hamburger buns; and a nose covered with a paper cup. He magically pulled hamburgers from behind his burger-shaped belt buckle. Who was this man?

124 Name the bald actor who played Jason Compson with an Eastern European accent in the 1959 film version of Faulkner's *The Sound and the Fury*.

125 How did blues singer Huddie Ledbetter (1885–1949) come to be known as "Leadbelly"?

126 What traveling tent show manager became Elvis Presley's manager?

127 "Rumble" (1958) was a hit song by what three brothers from Dunn, North Carolina?

LITERATURE

The presence alone of Faulkner in our midst makes a great difference in what the writer can and cannot permit himself to do. Nobody wants his mule and wagon stalled on the same track the Dixie Limited is roaring down. – Flannery O'Connor, Mystery and Manners

1 What 1957 novel dealt with violence, lust, racism, and miscegenation on the fictional Alabama plantation Falconhurst?

2 What character, in what 1947 play, says "I have always depended on the kindness of strangers"?

3 What animal trickster in African American folklore outwitted a fox?

4 What 1941 book described the lives of three Alabama tenant families in intimate detail?

5 What book series grew out of the work of students at Georgia's Rabun Gap–Nacoochee School, who collected oral histories of their relatives?

6 John Crowe Ransom, Donald Davidson, Allen Tate, and Robert Penn Warren were the core members of what literary movement?

7 What two well-known Mississippi writers were employed by the Federal Writers' Project in the 1930s?

8 Born Augustus Washington Bailey, this slave escaped to freedom and adopted a new surname from the hero of Sir Walter Scott's *Lady of the Lake*. He later wrote what is generally considered the classic slave autobiography.

9 Who wrote *The Autobiography of Miss Jane Pittman*?

10 What 1974 memoir of a black Alabama sharecropper made the *New York Times* best-seller list?

11 What was the title of the celebrated memoir by minister and social activist Will Campbell, in which he describes his poor white background, his developing interest in civil rights, and his brother's decline and death?

12 What African American writer from Augusta, Georgia, wrote popular romance novels like *The Foxes of Harrow* (1946),

which were set in the antebellum South and helped popularize the notion of the Old South as a land of moonlight and magnolias?

13 Who wrote *Cane*, a sensual portrayal of black life that emphasized folk culture and experimented with jazz forms and modern literary techniques?

14 What is the oldest literary quarterly in America?

15 Two controversial novels were set at The Citadel, a famous military college in Charleston. Name the novels and their authors.

16 What best-selling novelist was struck and killed by a speeding taxicab as she crossed Peachtree Street in Atlanta?

17 What North Carolina journalist published his brilliant book *The Mind of the South* in 1941 and took his own life later the same year?

18 We hear a lot about the Protestant South, but many of its best writers have been Catholics. Name three southern Catholic writers.

19 According to Harry Crews, the "Wish Book" brought "all that color and all that mystery and all that beauty into the lives of country people." What was the "Wish Book"?

20 What 1944 best-seller, set in Georgia, portrayed a clandestine love affair between an educated young black woman and the son of a white doctor?

21 What fictional Louisiana demagogue said, "Man is conceived in sin and born in corruption, and he passeth from the stink of the didie to the stench of the shroud"?

22 What novel, written in response to the Fugitive Slave Law of 1850, portrays the antebellum South as beautiful but tragically flawed and debilitated by the evils of slavery?

23 What well-known nineteenth-century jurist published twenty-six sketches and satires depicting ignorant, inept, and crafty judges and attorneys and their tacky clients?

24 Who was the first African American to publish a book in the South?

25 What eastern Tennessee writer wrote screenplays for the films *The African Queen* and *The Night of the Hunter*?

26 Harriette Arnow (b. 1908), a Kentucky novelist, centered her most popular book on Gertie Nevels, a woman whose life changes drastically when she and her husband and five children move from a Kentucky tenant farm to an urban housing development in wartime Detroit. What is the title of the book?

27 Among Maryland writer John Barth's well-known works is a novel based on the life of Ebenezer Cooke (1667–post 1732), the poet laureate of colonial Maryland. What is the novel?

28 What contemporary fictional character had a job peddling hot dogs in the French Quarter of New Orleans?

29 What Georgia poet, a fighter pilot in the Pacific in World War II, won the National Book Award for poetry and served as poetry consultant at the Library of Congress from 1966 to 1968?

30 What African American writer published a militant and highly inspirational poem called "For My People" (1942) and a novel titled *Jubilee* (1966)?

31 From what famous poem are these lines taken?

> All down the hills of Habersham
> All through the valleys of Hall,
> The rushes cried *Abide, abide*
> The willful waterweeds held me thrall.

32 Though he is considered the quintessential southern playwright, his plays include almost no blacks, and none prominently.

33 Who lived at the P.O. in China Grove, Mississippi?

34 In 1940, when she was only twenty-three, Georgian Lula Carson Smith published her first novel. What was her pen name, and what was the novel called?

35 What English novelist toured America in 1842 and later wrote of a steamboat journey from Cincinnati to Louisville, where he encountered a Choctaw representative to Washington?

36 What writer published five novels before completing his masterpiece, a three-volume history of the Civil War?

37 What Virginia colonist kept a "Secret Diary" that recorded daily life in Tidewater Virginia in intimate detail, including such events as a reconciliatory "flourish" of his wife on a billiard table?

38 Where did Erskine Caldwell's characters Lov Bensey, Jeeter, Ellie May, Dude, and Pearly Lester live?

39 What Kentucky poet, essayist, and novelist, whose work is characterized by dry wit and strong pacifist and agrarian themes, has won many national awards?

40 Born in 1885, half-blind, ninety-nine years old, locked in a charity home, Lucy Marsden is the central character in what 1989 best-seller?

41 What two southern poets penned famous odes to fallen Confederate soldiers?

42 What poet was an editor at *Vanity Fair* from 1920 to 1922, a suitor of Edna St. Vincent Millay, and a lifelong friend of Edmund Wilson and F. Scott Fitzgerald?

43 What eminent Kentucky scholar and Yale professor joined Robert Penn Warren and others in 1935 to found the *Southern Review*?

44 In this 1988 Pulitzer Prize–winning play and 1990 film starring Jessica Tandy and Morgan Freeman, who did Hoke drive?

45 Who could not go home again, and where was home?

46 Who went "north toward home" to become editor of *Harper's Magazine* from 1967 to 1971?

47 What writer of vastly popular children's books, including *Little Lord Fauntleroy* (1886) and *A Little Princess* (1905), lived near Knoxville, Tennessee?

48 In what novel did an unnamed protagonist remember his father's advice that to survive in a white man's world you must "yes'em to death"?

49 On what "real-life person" did Harper Lee base the character Dill in *To Kill a Mockingbird* (1960)?

50 In 1956, Flannery O'Connor wrote to a friend about the "feminist business," "I suppose I divide people into two classes: the Irksome and the Non-Irksome without regard to sex. Yes and there are the Medium Irksome and the Rare Irksome." What is the title of the 1979 collection that contains this letter and others by O'Connor?

51 What institution holds an annual Elvis conference and a Faulkner conference?

52 Admiral Dewey, Watkins Products, Wallstreet Panic, Montgomery Ward, and Mink are members of what famous fictional family?

53 What Georgia writer has written novels on gospel singers and snake handlers, among other southern subjects?

54 Who was Stingo, and who was his woman of choice?

55 What Tennessee writer and student of the Fugitives wrote subtle and beautifully reserved stories exploring the complicated relationships within "good" old southern families and between the different sections of his native state?

56 What prolific Virginia novelist, rumored to have murdered a relative, wrote *Jurgen* (1919), a controversial "modern" novel?

57 What 1974 book, which sold two million hardcover copies in three years and spawned a twelve-hour television miniseries, sparked new interest in African American genealogy?

58 Historically known as a magazine graveyard, the South produces four periodicals with circulations of one million or more. Name them.

59 What English actress and writer married southern planter Pierce Butler in 1834 but was horrified by the slavery practiced on his rice plantation and divorced him in 1848?

60 There have been two writing Thomas Wolfes. Which one wrote *The Electric Kool-Aid Acid Test* (1968)?

61 What writer, born in Hillsboro, West Virginia, is thus far the only woman to win both a Pulitzer Prize and the Nobel Prize for literature?

62 What poet, who spent part of her childhood in Arkansas, recited a poem at Arkansas native Bill Clinton's presidential inauguration in January 1993, and what was the poem's title?

63 Who was Deacon Lunchbox?

64 What small-town attorney became the best-selling writer in the world?

65 Cross Creek, in the north central Florida scrub country, was the home of what author?

66 According to novelist Pat Conroy, what town is "the Vatican City of Southern Letters"?

67 Where does drag queen Lady Chablis entertain?

68 What do Howard O'Brien, Anne Rice, Anne Rampling, and A. N. Roquelaure have in common?

69 What literary figure was known as "the Corncob Man"?

70 Match the writer with his or her alter ego.

William Styron	Scout Finch
Walker Percy	Eugene Gant
Robert Penn Warren	Will Barrett
Harper Lee	Richard
Thomas Wolfe	Stingo
Richard Wright	Jack Burden

71 What Florida writer, who studied with anthropologist Franz Boas in the 1920s, wrote *Mules and Men*, a collection of black folkways and religious practices?

SCIENCE, MEDICINE, BUSINESS, AND INDUSTRY

Move from Bentonville? That would be the last thing we [would] do unless they run us out. The best thing we ever did was to hide back there in the hills and eventually build a company that makes folks want to find us. They get there sometimes with a lot of trepidation and problems, but we like where we are. It's because of the work ethic, because of the chemistry of the people up there and the support we get. We're much better off than if we had gone to Chicago.
– Sam Walton, founder of Wal-Mart

1 What technological innovation has changed the nature of southern life most dramatically?

2 Peanuts, nutritious legumes that have figured large in southern culture since colonial times, are popularly known as "goobers." How did the name originate?

3 What modern airline began in 1924 as a crop-dusting business and grew to be the first commercial carrier to inaugurate DC-8, DC-9, and Convair 880 service?

4 What Texas metropolis is known as Space City?

5 What Louisiana university was originally founded in 1834 by seven physicians seeking to create a medical college to study and combat cholera and yellow fever?

6 In 1951, Kemmons Wilson (b. 1913) founded a motel chain in Memphis, Tennessee, that eventually became the largest of its kind in the country. What was it?

7 What killed 50 to 90 percent of Native Americans during the sixteenth through eighteenth centuries?

8 Where was the first forestry school in the nation established?

9 What 1793 invention made cotton growing commercially viable?

10 What disease, usually associated with the tropics, repeatedly ravaged the Gulf states and the lower Mississippi Valley during the nineteenth century?

11 Where is the National Leprosarium located?

12 One-fifth of Mississippi's entire revenue in 1866 was spent for these necessities for the returning soldiers. What were they?

13 Joseph Goldberger of the United States Public Health Service blamed the prevalence of this disease on the southerner's "Three-M Diet" of meat, meal, and molasses.

14 One of the first commercially important crops in South Carolina was established there in the seventeenth century with seed imported from Madagascar. What was it?

15 The early southern economy depended on what four basic staple crops?

16 What was the strongest formal argument for black inferiority published by an American before the nineteenth century?

17 What disease devastated Nashville in 1873?

18 Playing on the initials and the inefficiency of southern railroads, what lines did the following nicknames describe: the God-Forgotten; the Can't and Never-Will; and Hell Either Way You Take It?

19 What Alabama town was planned as a new industrial center by New South boosters in the late nineteenth century?

20 What four states have the lowest life expectancies in the nation?

21 Tobacco chewing has been a peculiarly American form of tobacco use, so much so that nineteenth-century English traveler Charles Mackay thought the national symbol for the United States should be not the eagle but this common household furnishing.

22 What shocking experiment was conducted by the U.S. Public Health Service in Macon County, Alabama, from the 1920s until 1972?

23 Who established the Frontier Nursing Service in the Kentucky mountains in 1925?

24 What agricultural educator, born into slavery in southwest Missouri, is best known for his attempts to find commercial uses for such southern crops as peanuts and sweet potatoes?

25 What was the first southern educational institution for the deaf?

26 What nineteenth-century leader in "scientific racism" published the authoritative American text on racial differences?

27 What root is used in voodoo conjuring to treat everything from dysentery to impotence?

28 True or false?: Cotton was king in the Old South. In 1860, the value of the cotton crop far outstripped the value of all other crops produced.

29 What is byssinosis?

30 Where did Dr Pepper get its name?

31 What railroad was the first steam-powered line in the South?

32 What Danville, Kentucky, pioneer in abdominal surgery is believed to have died of acute appendicitis?

33 What mass-market, overnight delivery business is based in Memphis?

34 What drink, now consumed by athletes all over the world, was first developed by a University of Florida kidney specialist?

35 What is pneumoconiosis?

36 Georgian Ray Charles's favorite soft drink was first concocted in 1896 by Caleb Bradham, a pharmacist in New Bern, North Carolina. Which one is it?

37 Who was surgeon general of the Confederate Army?

38 What medical investigator traveled to Cuba to search for the origins of yellow fever and identified the *Aedes aegypti* mosquito as its carrier?

39 What North Carolina philanthropist made his fortune on tobacco and electric power and endowed a major university?

40 What famous brand of coffee, advertised by the early muppets Wilkins and Wontkins, was first roasted and blended in Nashville around 1880?

41 Favorite strains of the largest crop grown in the South today are named for Confederate heroes: Davis, Lee, Forrest, Pickett, Jackson, Bragg, and Rebel. What is the crop?

42 In 1935, fewer than 4 percent of southern farms had what modern convenience?

43 Under whose leadership did Florida develop a thriving economy built on tourism, citrus, and specialized agriculture?

44 What favorite southern condiment is produced on Louisiana's Avery Island?

45 What 285-foot-long, 58-foot-wide paddlewheel steamer regularly makes the trip from Cincinnati to New Orleans?

46 What is geophagy?

47 What pest has caused nearly $59 million in damage to soybean crops over the years?

48 What state is the nation's largest producer of Christmas trees?

49 First mixed in a three-legged pot and stirred with an oar, what popular drink was developed as a hangover cure?

50 What chain of southern grocery stores was founded by Clarence Saunders (1881–1953) of Memphis?

51 In what state is the only commercially produced tea in America grown?

52 What was Hadacol?

53 What discount chain began in Arkansas in the 1960s and now has over 2,216 stores?

54 In 1984, which two states led in the sale of manufactured (mobile) homes?

55 What is the largest tobacco company in America?

56 Cotton cultivation used to define the Deep South, but where is the majority of today's cotton crop grown?

57 Which state produces the most tobacco?

58 What is the busiest port in the United States?

59 What "finger-lickin' good" franchise began in the back room of a filling station in Corbin, Kentucky, in the 1930s?

60 How did the southern grocery store chain Jitney Jungle get its name?

61 What nasty critter, a standard item in the colonial-era doctor's bag, is still used today by reconstructive surgeons?

62 What phenomenally popular toy was born in Babyland General Hospital in Cleveland, Georgia?

63 How many bourbon distilleries are currently operating in Bourbon County, Kentucky: 673, 154, 26, or 0?

64 What was involved in the "Slater system," which southern mills relied on for many years?

65 What city was the first in the nation to register and periodically inspect prostitutes?

66 Where can one experience multi-G forces, a simulated journey to Jupiter, a space shuttle landing, and being shot thirty feet into the air?

67 What distillery seals its bourbon with distinctive drippy red wax and is listed as a National Historic Landmark – the only operating distillery with such an honor?

68 Corvettes are made in only one place in the world. Where is it?

69 What industry, located in Spring Hill, Tennessee, has a world-wide reputation for throwing lavish homecoming parties, organizing family socials, protecting the environment, farming soybeans, and building playgrounds for neighborhood children?

70 The nation's top three steel producers are in the North, but the fourth is a southern company. What is this company and where is it located?

71 What chain of restaurants, based in Lebanon, Tennessee, has over two hundred locations in twenty-three states and describes a visit to its stores as "like traveling back to an era when stopping on the road for a meal was special. Out front there's a welcoming front porch filled with cozy rocking chairs"?

72 What airline has enhanced its planes with a portrait of Elvis and B. B. King's guitar to promote special fares on their birthdays?

73 Where is fiery Texas Pete chili sauce manufactured: Winston-Salem, North Carolina; Dry Prong, Louisiana; Texas, Kentucky; or Petersburg, Texas?

ART AND ARCHITECTURE

The South is almost as sterile, artistically, intellectually, culturally, as the Sahara Desert. . . . In all that gargantuan paradise of the fourth rate there is not a single picture gallery worth going into, or a single orchestra capable of playing the nine symphonies of Beethoven, or a single opera-house, or a single theater devoted to decent plays. . . . When you come to critics, musical composers, painters, sculptors, architects and the like, you will have to give it up, for there is not even a bad one between the Potomac mud-flats and the Gulf.
– *H. L. Mencken,* New York Evening Mail, *1917*

1 Established in North Carolina in 1933, this art school's faculty included some of the most influential architects and artists of the twentieth century. What was the name of the school?

2 Whose photographs documented the horrors of the Civil War and revolutionized war reportage?

3 What Englishman created many delicate watercolor renderings of New World flora, fauna, and Native American life as draftsman and cartographer to Sir Walter Raleigh's 1585 expedition?

4 Sherwood Forest, located in Charles City County, Virginia, was home to which U.S. president?

5 What school, still in existence, was founded on the model of the Scandinavian folk school as an alternative to the traditional rural school?

6 What Mississippi artist, best known for his baroque-style paintings depicting African American life, was awarded a Guggenheim Fellowship in 1939?

7 In 1853, Ann Pamela Cunningham of Charleston, South Carolina, began the quest to save what historic home?

8 Conceived in the 1920s with the notion of its benefactor, John D. Rockefeller, "that the future may learn from the past," this re-created colonial community annually receives one million paying visitors and two million nonpaying visitors.

9 What nineteenth-century English artist moved to Charleston at the age of nine and later painted a portrait of Queen Victoria?

10 What photographer was hired in 1907 to photograph the tragedy of child labor abuses in the textile mills and fishing industries of the South?

11 What is the name of the birthplace of Robert E. Lee: Carter's Grove, Bremo, Stratford Hall, or Gunston Hall?

12 What contemporary artist and photographer from Hale County, Alabama, returns there to continue a photographic record begun by Walker Evans in *Let Us Now Praise Famous Men*?

13 What college developed an extensive art training program for women, including a thriving pottery?

14 Typical of Greek Revival architecture, this architectural feature practically epitomizes the Old South. What is it?

15 Where is the world's largest mass of exposed granite?

16 Beauvoir, located in Biloxi, Mississippi, was home to which southern politician?

17 In this country, the distinctly southern alkaline glaze on stoneware pottery was likely first developed in what part of the South?

18 In the late eighteenth and early nineteenth centuries, a unique urban dwelling developed in Charleston, South Carolina. It is characterized by a long, narrow, often only one-room-wide plan and an entranceway through a doorway onto a two-story porch or piazza. What is the common name for this house type?

19 What university was designed by Thomas Jefferson, who also planned its innovative curriculum and recruited its mostly European faculty?

20 What city has architect Michael Graves's pyramidal Humana Tower, one of the nation's foremost examples of postmodern architecture?

21 In the 1890s, what famous cultural observer and architect designed the landscapes of the Biltmore Estate and Atlanta's Druid Hills area?

22 One of the most skilled and famous contemporary southern artisans is Philip Simmons of Charleston, South Carolina. What medium does he work in?

23 What Baltimore artist was the first professional African American painter in the European tradition?

24 What is often described as the best example of Palladian-style architecture in the South?

25 What regionalist painter traveled the back roads of the Deep South in 1928 and 1929 gathering material for murals like *The Arts of the South*?

26 What historic residence was the first home to be owned by the federal government?

27 What contemporary Arkansas architect designed the lovely Thorncrown Chapel in Eureka Springs?

28 What French Impressionist painter spent 1872 and 1873 visiting kin in New Orleans?

29 What contemporary resort near Point Washington, Florida, has been carefully planned to capture the atmosphere of a small southern town around the turn of the century?

30 Who was the "Mad Potter of Biloxi"?

31 What African American from Charlotte, North Carolina, one of the greatest American artists of the twentieth century, said, "I paint out of the tradition of the Blues, of call and recall"?

32 What southern folk house type features a central hall open to the elements on both the front and rear entrances?

33 Who founded and designed the city of Savannah, Georgia?

34 What is the name of President Andrew Jackson's home?

35 In what region is the craft of coil-grass basketry, using sweetgrass, pine needles, and palmetto, still practiced, but now primarily for commercial gain?

36 What two great American artists were from Port Arthur, Texas?

37 Where is the only museum in the nation dedicated to exhibiting and researching the regional decorative arts of the early South?

38 Who designed the Virginia state capitol in Richmond?

39 This famous southern self-taught artist was once a bicycle repairman. One day, while painting a bike, he saw a face in a dab of paint, and it told him, "Paint sacred art." Who is he?

40 What is the oldest surviving brick building in the southern English colonies?

41 Where does one find French-influenced plantation houses characterized by wide two-story porticoes or galleries that often completely surround the house?

42 "Rice beds" – or poster beds decorated with carvings of bending heads of grain, interpreted as rice – are generally associated with what region?

43 What Atlanta architect is best known for his hotel designs featuring large central atriums, spectacular in their vertical dimension and surrounded by shops, restaurants, and lounges?

44 What Nashvillian is well-known in the art world for his zany, cartoonish painted constructions like *Ruckus Manhattan*?

45 "Cracker house" is the term given to the type of houses constructed by early settlers in what state?

46 What city hosts the annual Roadside Attractions Artists Parade, which features a ball, a symposium, and a competition for the most spectacular art car?

47 What well-known South Carolina artist may be best known for his beer can images?

48 What automotive part is commonly used as a decorative planter?

49 What dried vegetable is often used to make bird nests throughout the South?

SPORTS AND RECREATION

It is no doubt a cliché, yet true, that Southern football is a religion, and many Southern football heroes have achieved a sort of civil sainthood.
– Willie Morris

1 Who was the first black tennis player to win a major national tournament?

2 What illegal sport is sometimes referred to as the "sport of kings"?

3 In what year did Jackie Robinson of Georgia break the color line in baseball?

4 Mississippi College students and alumni are known as what?

5 Two of the three Triple Crown races are held in southern states. Name them and their locations.

6 Participants in this 1970s craze were "excluded from prosecution" by the state of Louisiana if they "did not attempt to arouse the sexual desires of their viewers." What was the craze?

7 When this black jockey, who won the Kentucky Derby three times, died in 1896, his estate was worth $50,000. Who was he?

8 What golfer – described by commentator Alistair Cooke as "a gentleman, a combination of goodness and grace, an unwavering courtesy, self-deprecation, and consideration for other people" – in 1950 won the British Amateur, the British Open, the U.S. Open, and the U.S. Amateur?

9 What does NASCAR stand for?

10 According to many Tar Heels, what color is the sky?

11 In Tuscaloosa, what is the tide known to do?

12 What university's mascot is traditionally an animal used in an illegal sport?

13 Where was the National Tobacco Spitting Contest once held?

14 What fish is the king of all freshwater game fish in the South because it is widely distributed, easy but not too easy to catch, and tastes good?

15 Mobile, Alabama, has produced several great baseball players. Name three of them.

16 What Georgia baseball hero, who once described himself as "a snarling wildcat," retired with a lifetime batting average of .367?

17 Name three Tennessee theme parks that take their names from country music singers.

18 What Arkansas baseball player retired to become a broadcaster and entertained listeners with his hillbilly vernacular, which included terms like "slud," "swang," "pressperation," "airs" (errors), and "spart" (spirit)?

19 What was the first 500-mile stock car race to be broadcast live on television in its entirety?

20 What sporting event occurs on the first Saturday in May and is always celebrated with mint juleps, roses, and steamboat and balloon races?

21 What university has an arachnid as its mascot?

22 When and where was fox hunting probably first enjoyed in the southern states?

23 "Hotty Toddy, Goshamighty, Who in the hell are we?"

24 What was the last Division I college to allow African Americans to play on its basketball team?

25 What Tar Heel basketball coach initiated a distinctive "four corners" offensive style?

26 Match the following coaches with the college teams where they had their greatest successes:

Paul "Bear" Bryant	Clemson
Eddie Robinson	Georgia Tech
John Heisman	Grambling
Bob Neyland	Alabama
Frank Howard	Tennessee

27 What Floridian, widely enjoyed for his folksy, intelligent, and gentlemanly broadcasts, was for many years the broadcaster for the Brooklyn Dodgers and then later for the New York Yankees?

28 What supercharged boy from Ingle Hollow, North Carolina, perfected his "bootleg" turns in the mountains and hollows of Wilkes County while running moonshine and went on to become a legendary champion stock car racer?

29 What woman from Port Arthur, Texas, a top golfer and a star of the 1932 Olympic Games, is still considered the greatest American woman athlete?

30 What Randolph County, North Carolina, family is a stock car racing dynasty?

31 What college football player, originally from the Mississippi Delta, in 1970 set a Southeastern Conference record for total offense in a single game – 540 yards, including thirty-three completions out of fifty-two pass attempts?

32 What is the distance of the Kentucky Derby?

33 In what northern game, adopted by the South and absorbed fully into its culture, do southern boys regularly outperform the original innovators?

34 What university's mascot is the moccasin?

35 What is the longest superspeedway on the NASCAR circuit?

36 Who was the first black heavyweight champion?

37 Who was the first black golfer to participate in the Masters Tournament in Augusta, Georgia?

38 What two world-renowned athletes, one an Olympic champion track star and the other a boxer, were both sons of Alabama sharecroppers and were born only months apart?

39 Where is the Dixie National Baton Twirling Institute held?

40 In 1960, professional football arrived in the South with what two teams?

41 What southern university's football stadium is called Death Valley?

42 Match these Atlantic Coast Conference team mascots with their teams:

University of Maryland	Tar Heels
University of North Carolina	Yellow Jackets
Duke University	Wolfpack
Wake Forest University	Terrapins
Georgia Tech	Seminoles
North Carolina State University	Cavaliers
Clemson University	Demon Deacons
Florida State University	Blue Devils
University of Virginia	Tigers

43 Who was the first football player from the South to be named All-American?

44 What is often called the Redneck Riviera?

45 Who is the winningest coach in college football?

46 The annual award for the best college football player is named for what man?

47 What is bourré (pronounced BOO-ray)?

48 Where is the Arlington Hotel?

49 What was the name of Louisiana's Class D minor league, sometimes known as baseball's "hot pepper circuit"?

50 Who is the only African American to win both the U.S. Open and Wimbledon?

51 What city in Florida is known for breeding thoroughbred horses?

52 Originally named after an abolitionist, this Kentuckian was stripped of his boxing title for his refusal to serve in the Vietnam War.

53 What coach established the North Carolina Tar Heels as a national basketball power in the 1950s before moving on to become the basketball coach and athletic director of the University of South Carolina?

54 Where is the Richard Petty Museum?

55 What takes place on the first Saturday in October in Irmo, South Carolina?

56 What was the greatest skunk in college football history?

57 What Arkansas-born Southeastern Conference football coach won thirteen SEC and six national championships?

58 What does the term "happy hour" refer to in Winston Cup racing?

59 What resort lying near Charleston, South Carolina, lures over 700,000 annual visitors with its semitropical temperatures, six marinas, seventeen golf courses, two hundred–plus tennis courts, white sand beaches, nature trails, and an assortment of wildlife?

60 Who held the world checkers championship title from 1955 until his death in 1995?

61 The score "6–0" was once displayed on walls, rocks, and other outdoor places in Kentucky. What does it signify?

62 Who was known as the "Baron of Barlow Bend"?

63 Who are the Rattlers?

64 Other than Kentucky, only one SEC school has won three consecutive regular season basketball titles. What is the school, and in what years did it win?

65 What major league pitcher, playing for what team, hit two grand slam home runs in one game?

66 Danny Ford and Ken Hatfield have served as head football coaches for the same ACC and SEC schools. Name the two schools.

67 Who were the Pelicans, Travelers, Chicks, Vols, Lookouts, Crackers, Barons, and Bears?

68 In what state is the annual pirogue race held?

69 Wading into deep water, sticking an arm into a hollow, submerged log hoping to wrestle a catfish and not a water moccasin is a method of fishing known as what?

70 Who was the only woman driver to compete in the first-ever NASCAR-sanctioned stock car race?

71 Where is the Greenbrier?

72 What SEC football team plays "between the hedges"?

73 From 1991 to 1993, what college team mounted Shaq Attacks?

74 The South produced the play that made the modern game of football possible. What was it?

75 What was one of Cal Ripken Jr.'s earliest jobs in professional baseball?

76 What are dog trials?

77 From 1978 to 1986, a six-foot, 450-pound Georgia pig farmer won more than fifty world titles in this sport. What sport is it?

THE LAND

Unlike time, place has surface, which will take the imprint of man – his hand, his foot, his mind; it can be tamed, domesticated. It has shape, size, boundaries; man can measure himself against them. It has atmosphere and temperature, change of light and show of season, qualities to which man spontaneously responds. Place has always nursed, nourished, and instructed man; he in turn can rule it and ruin it, take it and lose it, suffer if he is exiled from it, and after living on it he goes to it in his grave. – Eudora Welty, The Eye of the Story

1 What infamous insect is lamented in a Leadbelly song and honored with a monument in Enterprise, Alabama?

2 What is the "Father of Waters"?

3 What is the "Bluff City"?

4 What is the name of the old Indian trail running in a southwesterly direction from Nashville to the Mississippi River?

5 What geological feature in present-day Mason and Boone Counties, Kentucky, attracted countless buffalo and other animals in the time before human habitation?

6 Who built the Wilderness Road, and where did it go?

7 What New Deal program, begun to provide jobs, electricity, better land management, and flood control in the Middle South, is also credited with eradicating malaria in that region?

8 Because of the Interstate system, many southern cities are ringed with superhighways, but only one of these highways is known as "the Beltway." What is it?

9 Name the three major species of catfish found in the South.

10 What southern port city was named for the Maubila Indians?

11 What aromatic southern tree, now valued by homemakers for protection against wool-eating insects, did Cherokee Indians regard as sacred?

12 What city was both the "Cradle of the Confederacy" and the birthplace of the modern civil rights movement?

13 Of what body of water, the largest estuary in North America, did Captain John Smith say, "Heaven and earth never agreed better to frame a place for man's habitation"?

14 What Chesapeake town claims the title "Blue Crab Capital of the World"?

15 What is the Big Thicket?

16 What two colonies did the Mason-Dixon Line separate?

17 What scavenging, nocturnal marsupial should we all eat more of, according to its 40,000-strong Growers and Breeders Association, based in Clanton, Alabama?

18 This mountain range gets its name from the persistent blue haze that hangs over its peaks. What is it?

19 Where is the "Graveyard of the Atlantic"?

20 Journalist James J. Kilpatrick considered this plant a metaphor for the South, "an indigenous, an indestructible part of the Southern character; it blurs, conceals, softens, wraps the hard limbs of hard times in a fringed shawl." What was he talking about?

21 What is the "Tenn-Tom"?

22 What 1927 disaster in Mississippi and Louisiana was chronicled in William Alexander Percy's *Lanterns on the Levee*?

23 What southern tree has knees?

24 What state is the top exporter of collard greens?

25 What plant, cultivated in the Orient for two thousand years, was imported in the 1930s to help control erosion in the South?

26 What flowering tree, often associated with the Deep South, is the official state flower of Louisiana and Mississippi?

27 It was said, in the early twentieth century, that one-sixth of the world's wealth gathered each winter on this Georgia barrier island.

28 Over one-half of what hazardous waste is stored in the South?

29 What city, the "Athens of the South," has a replica of the Parthenon?

30 What Florida city, established as an army post in 1824, prospered in the nineteenth and early twentieth centuries, first as a center of cattle trade with Cuba and later as the center of the cigar industry?

31 True or false?: Florida has more Atlantic shoreline than any other southern state.

32 For what southern state is the lowest point *below* sea level?

33 What state was the most populous in the first census of 1790?

34 True or false?: According to average high temperatures in July, measured over three decades (1950–1980), none of the Deep South states is among the five hottest states in the United States.

35 In 1923, nonresidents owned more than one-half of this southern state and controlled four-fifths of its total value.

36 What vegetable has been used by southerners to staunch bleeding, make coarse cloth or paper, adorn dried flower arrangements, clean metal, unstop drains, increase the milk yield of cows, and provide a coffee and plasma substitute?

37 These "walls," built to repel annual invasion, are longer than the Great Wall of China. What are they?

38 Where are the Piney Woods?

39 In 1893, the Florida legislature passed the first bill to protect this aquatic mammal, whose nearest relative is the elephant.

40 What is the Vieux Carré?

41 What two birds are now extinct but were once so common in the South that they were regarded as pests?

42 What is the name for the region of rolling hills that divides the mountains and coastal plain in the South Atlantic states?

43 What are Callaway, Bellingrath, Cypress, Hodges, Magnolia, and Brookgreen?

44 What Florida lake is the second largest freshwater lake that lies wholly within the United States?

45 What is the name of the 300-mile-long area of rich, dark, fertile soil that stretches across central Alabama and northeastern Mississippi and into Tennessee?

46 What happened in the Mississippi Valley on December 16, 1811, creating new lakes and causing the Mississippi River to change direction?

47 What natural disaster struck Galveston, Texas, on September 8, 1900, taking the lives of 6,000 of the city's 20,000 residents?

48 What is a "chicken choker"?

49 What Tennessee city's name is derived from an Indian expression meaning "a rock rising to a point"?

50 What is a "snake doctor" or "skeeter hawk"?

51 What is brailing?

52 What Caribbean island nation gave the South shotgun houses, Marie Laveau, and regular dramatic performances in New Orleans?

53 What is the highest point in the Appalachian Mountains?

54 Besides the Everglades, what are the largest swamps in the South?

55 What infamous pirate used the sounds and bays behind the Outer Banks of North Carolina as a hiding place in the 1700s?

56 Thomas Jefferson actually owned what natural wonder?

57 Where is the longest recorded cave system on earth?

58 What Kentucky town proclaims itself "Home of 2,000 Happy People and a Few Soreheads"?

59 What southern city is the only one in America named for a newspaper?

60 What is the oldest European settlement in the Louisiana Purchase?

61 Where is the largest naval base in the world?

62 What Florida city is the nation's second largest in area?

63 What natural disaster caused the Virginia legislature to change its missing persons law in 1970?

64 What man-made structure stretches 17.6 miles across the mouth of the Chesapeake Bay, from Cape Charles on the Eastern Shore of Virginia to Virginia Beach and Norfolk?

65 In what present-day city did the Jamestown settlers first land in 1607?

66 Which three Deep South states include both a Jefferson Davis County and a Lincoln County?

67 Which state uses parishes as opposed to counties as its municipal districts?

68 What parasite has been termed the southern "germ of laziness"?

69 The highest point of this rugged highland range is in the Boston Mountains.

70 What is the name of the early-nineteenth-century road that connected Washington, D.C., and New Orleans?

71 Where is the Wiregrass?

72 What is the "Perimeter"?

73 What is a loblolly?

74 In what state can you find a Climax and an Enigma?

75 This snake, the most poisonous one in America, is found in the southeastern states.

76 What is the name of the famous scenic road between Baton Rouge and New Orleans?

77 True or false?: Alligators, once an endangered species, are now common as far north as North Carolina.

78 Rebecca Lynn, of Jacksonville, Florida, recently won a visit from entomologist Austin Frishman, $1,000 in cash, and a year's supply of pest-control products. What distinction earned her this prize?

79 What city was named in 1765 for George III's wife?

80 Where are Pall Mall, Marlboro, and Chesterfield located?

81 In what city did Mardi Gras originate?

82 In the 1950s it was not unusual for a barn roof in the rural South to direct passersby to see what?

83 A visiting English naturalist, writing in the early eighteenth century, described this member of the Trombiculadae family as a "very troublesome Insect. . . . They penetrate the skin, under which they lay a bunch or bag of eggs . . . which endangers a mortification." Who was the naturalist, and what is the insect?

84 Where is the only diamond reserve in North America?

85 Of the five most dangerous highways in the entire United States, what two are located in the South?

HISTORY, POLITICS, AND LAW

The past is never dead. It's not even past.
– William Faulkner, Requiem for a Nun

1 What 1831 slave rebellion in Southampton County, Virginia, led to the deaths of nearly sixty white men, women, and children?

2 What brilliant and practical social reformer – and reluctant crusader – was editor and publisher of the *Atlanta Constitution*?

3 When is Martin Luther King Jr.'s birthday?

4 In the years following World War I, black southerners left the South at a staggering rate to seek a better life in the North. Approximately how many blacks migrated between 1916 and 1920: 5,000, 50,000, or 500,000?

5 Whose drawing room served as a salon for the Confederate elite, enabling her to create a fascinating record of her Civil War experiences in a series of diaries?

6 What was the "Trail of Tears"?

7 What percentage of Medal of Honor recipients for service in Vietnam were from the South: 11 percent, 29 percent, or 52 percent?

8 Who won a special election in 1973 to fill her missing husband's congressional seat?

9 What organization based in Monteagle, Tennessee, developed leadership in labor unions and community groups struggling for justice and social change?

10 What did future United States Supreme Court justice Oliver Wendell Holmes reportedly say to Abraham Lincoln when Lincoln became the only president of the United States ever to come under enemy fire while in office?

11 First heard at Manassas, and repeated in hundreds of charges throughout the Civil War, this was as much a part of the Rebel's fighting equipment as his rifle.

12 Whose Civil War strategy is neatly summed up in the phrase "Git thar fustest with the mostest"?

13 What was the New Orleans Screwman's Benevolent Association?

14 What South Carolina sisters, raised in an elite, slave-owning Charleston family, became Quakers and vehement abolitionists?

15 In the first decades of the twentieth century, the Good Roads Movement helped launch a road-building program that would unite the North and South and bring jobs and money into the region. What organization inspired the movement?

16 What Arkansas woman became a media favorite during the Watergate hearings by claiming she was drugged and forcibly prevented from speaking out on the involvement of her husband, a high-ranking Nixon administration official?

17 What do Maynard Jackson, Andrew Young, Richard Arrington, and Ernest "Dutch" Morial have in common?

18 On May 17, 1954, the United States Supreme Court unanimously ruled in five cases that "separate educational facilities are inherently unequal." Collectively, the rulings were known as what?

19 In September 1963, just days after the March on Washington, what event in Birmingham, Alabama, shattered the good feelings of Martin Luther King's "I Have a Dream" speech?

20 What college, which began as a Methodist liberal arts college, became the first land-grant institution in the South?

21 What was the first regional historical organization?

22 Since 1882, approximately 82 percent of these acts of vigilante terrorism have taken place in the South. What are they?

23 What president launched the War on Poverty in 1964?

24 What was a "pateroller"?

25 When is Robert E. Lee's birthday?

26 Who refused to go to the back of the bus on December 1, 1955, prompting the Alabama bus boycott that gave rise to the modern civil rights movement?

27 What well-oiled political machine dominated Memphis politics from the mid-1920s until the early 1950s?

28 Who were the Regulators?

29 What southern army base greeted its new trainees with a sign on its main gate that read "Birthplace of Combat Infantrymen for Vietnam"?

30 Americana, Brazil, is home to what group?

31 What paper was started by the Communist Party in 1930 as a means of enlisting rural southern workers?

32 Who was perhaps the loudest and most fervent New South booster in the years following the Civil War?

33 What was the only town in the seceding states to remain in Federal hands for the entire war?

34 Who founded the Association of Southern Women for the Prevention of Lynching in 1930?

35 What president of Columbia College, now Columbia University, taught at the University of Alabama and was president of the University of Mississippi from 1856 until 1861?

36 What South Carolina–born woman is founder and president of the Children's Defense Fund?

37 What is the "Invisible Empire"?

38 In the dark days of the early civil rights movement, what city earned a reputation as the "Johannesburg of America"?

39 Among the signers of the Declaration of Independence, whose autograph is the rarest and the most valuable?

40 Violence growing out of a strike in the textile mills of what North Carolina town took the life of the chief of police?

41 True or false?: Civil War antagonists Jefferson Davis and Abraham Lincoln began life in the same state.

42 What feminist born in Baton Rouge, Louisiana, became one of the most articulate and radical advocates for the women's movement from 1966 to 1972?

43 What historic event took place in Yorktown, Virginia?

44 Who was "Old Hickory"?

45 What is eminent southern historian C. Vann Woodward's first name?

46 Match the following southern demagogues with the states they hailed from:

Theodore Bilbo	Georgia
Tom Watson	South Carolina
Ben Tillman	Alabama
Huey Long	Mississippi
George Wallace	Louisiana

47 What was the "peculiar institution"?

48 By what nickname did Robert E. Lee's soldiers commonly call him in the first year of the war?

49 To what American city did President Eisenhower dispatch the 101st Airborne Division in 1957?

50 What Native American tribe joined the Confederate States of America?

51 What military leader's men were characterized, in popular legend, as "half horse, half alligator"?

52 What Alabama governor exclaimed, "Segregation now! Segregation tomorrow! Segregation forever!" in his 1962 inaugural address?

53 What do NAACP, SCLC, CORE, and SNCC have in common?

54 What state was the first to secede from the Union in 1860?

55 What southern socialist organization was begun in the Arkansas Delta in 1934?

56 What Kentucky county's name has become practically synonymous with the violence of mine labor disputes?

57 What were "Sherman's hairpins"?

58 What was the only CIO union that maintained its headquarters south of the Mason-Dixon line?

59 What was the first museum in America?

60 Who broke the color barrier at the University of Mississippi in 1962?

61 When did the last officially recognized Civil War veteran die?

62 Having been persecuted in Germany, this group established a settlement in Georgia, near Savannah, in 1734.

63 What percentage of enlistees in the professional armed forces are natives of the South?

64 While campaigning for president, he told southern audiences, "Come January we are going to have a president in the White House who doesn't speak with an accent."

65 In 1956, all but twenty-seven of the southerners in Congress signed a document in which they urged the states to resist integration. What was that document called?

66 What Mississippi politician, who once shot a black man on a Washington streetcar, advocated shipping twelve million black southerners "back" to Africa as a means of solving unemployment?

67 After 1948, southern Democrats who rejected the liberal leadership of their national party were called what?

68 What six-term Arkansas governor defied the federal government by preventing the integration of Little Rock Central High School?

69 What Alabama Wiregrass politician was a classic southern populist who continually fought the elite "big mules" in power and spoke against racial discrimination and for women's rights and better education and roads?

70 What Georgia political figure responded to criticism of her defense of lynching by advocating that one thousand blacks be lynched every week if necessary to prevent rape?

71 What United States official under Buchanan later headed Confederate clandestine activities in Canada and may have had dealings with John Wilkes Booth before the assassination of Abraham Lincoln?

72 What Georgian first attracted national attention in 1964, when he denied service to blacks in his fried chicken restaurant, the Pickrick, by brandishing a pistol and distributing ax handles to his supporters?

73 What Florida legislator "retired" from the U.S. Senate to the House of Representatives, where he became known as a champion of the rights of the elderly?

74 What is the only southern state that does not allow capital punishment?

75 What Spanish conquistador was buried in the Mississippi River?

76 Destitute post-Reconstruction farmers, both black and white, were forced into a crop-lien system to secure credit for food, equipment, seed, and necessities. What were these farmers called?

77 Who was secretary of war and secretary of state for the Confederacy?

78 This mother of a president preferred small-town life, enjoyed bourbon, admitted that the only luxury she wanted was a "good-looking car," and served in the Peace Corps in India from 1966 to 1968.

79 Two of ten World War II Relocation Authority camps for Japanese were located in the South. Where were they?

80 This backwoods frontiersman, who according to a popular song "kilt him a bar when he was only three," was elected to the Tennessee legislature and won congressional elections in 1827, 1829, and 1833.

81 What was Robert E. Lee's daddy's nickname?

82 These two men, presently senators from the same state, were cheerleaders at the same college.

83 Near the end of World War I, this heroic Tennessean single-handedly outshot an entire German machine-gun battalion and brought 132 German prisoners out of the Argonne Forest.

84 What Chattanoogan developed the *New York Times* into a great American newspaper?

85 The explosion of this steamboat on April 27, 1865, killed more than 1,500 people.

86 What nineteenth-century congressman from Edgefield, South Carolina, beat Massachusetts senator Charles Sumner insensible on the floor of the Senate chamber because of remarks the congressman considered slanderous?

87 What Creole Confederate commanded the attack on Fort Sumter and led forces at Bull Run, Shiloh, and Charleston?

88 Who said, "I'm sick and tired of being sick and tired"?

89 What philanthropic foundation, established in 1917, provided roughly $63 million to improve rural education, race relations, and the health of black southerners?

90 Who led a slave uprising in Charleston in 1822?

91 As of 1975, what state was the only one that permitted conjugal visits for married prisoners and provided cottages for this purpose?

92 In the Spanish-American War, what two Confederate veterans were appointed major generals?

93 Where was the first historic district in the United States?

94 Where did man first fly?

95 What was the last southern state to abolish chain gangs?

96 What presidential candidate, in a *Playboy* interview, admitted that he had "committed adultery in his heart many times"?

97 The 1798 Virginia Resolutions were intended to defend civil liberties and assert the right of states to declare Federalist-sponsored acts unconstitutional, but they later became the foundation of states'-rights doctrine. Who first put them forward?

98 In 1972, what two African Americans became the first southern blacks since 1898 to win congressional elections?

99 What ninety-two-year-old senator from South Carolina once wrestled another senator to the floor in an attempt to prevent a quorum?

100 By 1624, the Jamestown Colony was annually exporting 60,000 pounds of this crop to England, where its use had become a fad among London's elite.

101 "Farmer Gene" was the nickname of what Monroe County, Georgia, politician?

102 What South Carolina woman was a pioneer in the successful cultivation of indigo in the southern colonies?

103 How many times a year were soldiers on both sides of the Civil War officially expected to change their underwear?

104 What failed planter and businessman, rough, awkward, and defiant in manner, became the Virginia delegate to the First Continental Congress of 1774 and gave a fiery speech arguing for armed rebellion against England?

105 What University of Oklahoma football hero was born in Neshoba County, Mississippi, the same month that three civil rights workers were murdered there?

106 Founded in Tennessee, this journal was the first antislavery newspaper.

107 What New York shipping and railroad baron founded a southern Methodist university?

108 Who wrote the Declaration of Independence?

109 When did the first ship carrying Africans arrive in North America?

110 Who was the leading southern populist of the late nineteenth century?

111 Who was the only Confederate officer executed for war crimes?

112 The nation's first gold rush occurred in what state?

113 Where was Franklin Roosevelt's Little White House?

114 General Grant recalls the surrender of General Lee this way: "Whatever his feelings they were entirely concealed . . . but my own feelings . . . were sad and depressed. I felt like anything rather than rejoicing at the downfall of a foe who had fought so long and valiantly." Where and when did the surrender take place?

115 What was the second college created in British North America?

116 What Tennessee circuit-riding judge and secretary of state from 1933 to 1944 won the Nobel Peace Prize in 1945?

117 What five southern states have flags that are based partially or fully on Confederate banners?

118 What civil rights leader became U.S. ambassador to the United Nations in 1976?

119 What was the first submarine used for naval combat?

120 Before he became famous for burning Atlanta and marching to the sea, what southern university did William Tecumseh Sherman head?

121 Sam Ervin of North Carolina and John Stennis of Mississippi were the only members of the U.S. Senate to vote against submitting this proposed amendment to the states for ratification in 1972.

122 What two states still prevented women from voting in the general election of 1920, even after the Nineteenth Amendment had been ratified?

123 In this 1896 case, the U.S. Supreme Court upheld Jim Crow laws and the "separate but equal" doctrine that persisted until *Brown v. Board of Education* (1954).

124 Name the three-time presidential candidate who died immediately after serving as prosecuting attorney in the famous "Monkey Trial" in Dayton, Tennessee.

125 Before World War II, what southern college furnished the U.S. Army with more regular officers than West Point?

126 What southern city had the nation's first electric street railway, the first civilian pilot training school, and the first planned municipal airport?

127 What native of Morganton, North Carolina, wrote an autobiography titled *Preserving the Constitution* (1985)?

128 Stricken with "acute congestion" at nineteen months and left blind, deaf, and dumb, this Alabama native overcame her handicaps to become a writer, lecturer, and inspiration to millions.

129 Where was the first attempt at English settlement in North America?

130 Fourteen U.S. presidents were born in the South. Leaving aside the Virginians Washington, Jefferson, Madison, and Monroe, name seven of the remaining ten.

131 What outdoorsman served as the inspiration for the Boy Scouts of America?

132 Who founded the Tuskegee Normal and Industrial Institute, in Macon County, Alabama?

133 On July 7, 1969, Charles Evers was sworn in as the first African American mayor of a biracial town in Mississippi since Reconstruction. What was the name of the town?

134 What Arkansas senator took a dip in the Tidal Basin with a Foxe?

135 What act effectively ended slavery in the United States?

136 What Seminole Indian chief united members of his tribe against the U.S. government during the Seminole Wars?

137 What was "Alabama Fever"?

138 Who was the first African American ever to be elected governor?

139 What is the nation's oldest city?

140 What Arkansas politician, educator, and businessman served in the U.S. Senate from 1945 to 1974 and wrote *The Arrogance of Power*?

141 This tubercular dentist from Griffin, Georgia, became a notorious gambler and gunslinger of the Old West.

142 What is a yellow-dog Democrat?

143 Who was the only Alabama governor to be forced out of office for being convicted of a felony?

144 In what town did Michael Griffin, a member of an antiabortion organization, gun down Dr. David Gunn in March 1993?

145 Why was the southern countryside once dotted with "Impeach Earl Warren" signs in the 1950s and 1960s?

146 The death rate at the infamous hellhole prisoner of war camp at Andersonville, Georgia, established near the end of the war while the Confederacy was unable to feed and supply its own armies, was 40 percent. What was the death rate among Confederates held at the federal prisoner of war camp at Elmira, New York, in the midst of plenty: 6 percent, 14 percent, or 24 percent?

147 What did Mississippi judge Tom Brady call the day the U.S. Supreme Court announced its decision on *Brown v. Board of Education*?

148 How did dashing Major General Earl Van Dorn of Mississippi die?

149 What name is given to the 1968 event on the campus of South Carolina State College in which three black students were killed and twenty-seven others wounded by police gunfire?

150 What were the last words of popular Union general John Sedgwick?

151 Approximately what percentage of casualties in the Vietnam War were southerners: 5 percent, 20 percent, or 35 percent?

152 What member of the Cherokee tribe spent twelve years developing a written language for his people?

153 What and where is "the Free State of Jones"?

154 In 1974 Randy Newman recorded a song on the album *Good Old Boys* that discussed the Standard Oil Men and the Kingfish. Who was the Kingfish, and what song written by him did Newman record on the same album?

155 What Georgia politician has, on different occasions, uttered both these statements regarding the House of Representatives: "The House is a corrupt institution" and "I'm a creature of the House"?

156 What island was the site of the only formally planned town developed for freed slaves by the Union army?

157 The burning of Atlanta is perhaps the most lasting image of General William Tecumseh Sherman's March to the Sea, but what city was his real target?

158 Who was romantically involved with Pocahontas?

ANSWERS

MANNERS, MYTH, AND RELIGION

1 A mule.

2 K-Paul's Louisiana Kitchen, where blackened redfish is a popular dish.

3 An English-based Creole language developed by the descendants of enslaved Africans in the low country and on the sea islands of South Carolina and Georgia.

4 "Good old boy."

5 English peas. Just plain "peas" more often refers to field peas like black-eyed peas, crowder peas, or purple-hulled peas.

6 Bonnie Parker (1910–34) and Clyde Barrow (1909–34), who had killed at least twelve people in a two-year crime spree through Texas, Oklahoma, Missouri, Arkansas, and Louisiana.

7 Powdered dry sassafras leaves, used to thicken gumbo. Filé originated with Choctaws on the north shore of Lake Pontchartrain, who sent the product to New Orleans cooks.

8 The St. Cecilia Ball. Originally held three times a year, during January and February, it featured talented musicians and dancing and was conducted with "the greatest decorum."

9 The Devil. Of southerners, 86 percent believed in the Devil; of non-southerners, only 52 percent did.

10 African Methodist Episcopal.

11 Breaux Bridge, Louisiana.

12 In the pine forest and palmetto South, cattle herders used long rawhide strips that produced a loud cracking noise when popped over the heads of the animals. Those who employed these whips were known as "crackers."

13 A ghost or apparition. The word is often used to describe a scary-looking woman, as in, "She can put on all the Mary Kay she wants, but she's still going to look like a haint." Boo Radley in Harper Lee's *To Kill a Mockingbird* was thought to be a haint.

14 Salley, South Carolina, where 20,000 people gather each fall to celebrate chitlins and consume five tons of them.

15 Jerry Falwell (b. 1933), pastor of the Thomas Road Baptist Church in Lynchburg, Virginia.

16 The many debutante balls that are still held throughout the South.

17 Bourbon. About it, Walker Percy (1916–90) wrote an essay titled "Bourbon," first published in the December 1975 *Esquire* and later in *Signposts in a Strange Land* (1991), which included this passage:

> Not only should connoisseurs of Bourbon not read this article, neither should persons preoccupied with the perils of alcoholism, cirrhosis, esophageal hemorrhage, cancer of the palate, and so forth – all real enough dangers. I, too, deplore these afflictions. But, as between these evils and the aesthetic of Bourbon drinking, that is, the use of Bourbon to warm the heart, to reduce the anomie of the late twentieth century, to cut the cold phlegm of Wednesday afternoons, I choose the aesthetic.

18 The signifying monkey. This type of poetic recitation is known as a toast.

19 False. It was a spinoff of the *Progressive Farmer*, a newspaper founded in 1886 in North Carolina, dedicated to promoting a better rural way of life, more scientific agricultural techniques, and improved education for farm people. *Time, Inc.*, bought *Southern Living* in 1985.

20 Jonesborough, Tennessee.

21 Columbia, Tennessee, where thousands of mules were raised and traded each year. Will Rogers said about Columbia, "What the thoroughfare of Wall Street will do to you if you don't know what a stock is, Columbia will do to you if you don't know a mule. Maiden Lane, New York City, for diamonds, but Mule Street in Columbia for mules."

22 The nineteenth-century feud between the Hatfields and the McCoys, who lived in the isolated Tug River Valley along the West Virginia–Kentucky border.

23 Sigma Alpha Epsilon, founded in 1856 at the University of Alabama.

24 Alpha Delta Pi, founded in 1851 at Wesleyan College in Macon, Georgia.

25 "Creation science" or "scientific creationism." This belief holds that scientific evidence supports the biblical refutation of Darwinian evolution as an explanation for human existence.

26 Charlotte "Lottie" Moon (1840–1912). The Lottie Moon Christmas Offering is administered by the Women's Missionary Union of the Southern Baptist Convention.

27 The juice left over from the cooking of greens. This nectarlike liquor is often sopped with cornbread.

28 Wednesday, when businesses will sometimes close at noon.

29 According to writer Larry Brown, "Bluetick hounds are blue with specks or spots and have tremendously deep voices. They are probably some of the best fighters there are in all the hound breeds except for maybe Plotts, who are used primarily on bears. A bluetick has an extremely cold nose. He will find an old track and work it up, bawling once in a while, until he gets closer to the coon and then he will get 'hotter' and start barking more. Some may weigh as much as eighty pounds." Blueticks are Mr. Brown's personal favorite.

30 The country store, located at crossroads all across the South.

31 Storyville. Now covered by a federal housing project, the district lies just east of Canal Street and north of the French Quarter.

32 Atlanta, which was successful in its postwar efforts to project a positive urban image and attract growth and investment.

33 About 65 percent, as opposed to 44 percent of non-southerners. About 40 percent of all southerners own handguns.

34 Corn.

35 Black-eyed peas. It's also a good idea to have some collards, which are symbolic of "foldin' money."

36 Hoppin' John.

37 The Sazerac. Modern barmen substitute Pernod for the absinthe.

38 Montreat, in western North Carolina. Methodists gather at Lake Junaluska and Southern Baptists at Ridgecrest, both in the North Carolina mountains.

39 "Woman, lovely woman of the Southland." The toast continues, "We pledge our hearts and our lives to the protection of her virtue and chastity."

40 Juneteenth, celebrated June 19. On that day in 1865, after the Civil War, Major General Gordon Granger arrived in Galveston to command the Texas district and officially announced the freedom of slaves.

41 The Church of God in Christ.

42 A small, bob-tailed dog, usually white with black or brown spots and short hair. Feists resemble rat terriers somewhat and make excellent squirrel dogs. This is the sort of dog that Faulkner called "fyce" in "The Bear."

43 Africa.

44 Burma Shave. It might be touted this way:

> From Saskatoon
> To Alabam'
> You hear men praise
> The shave
> What am
> Burma Shave

Burma Shave was not a southern company, but the signs were particularly popular in the South because of the abundance of suitable rural roads. Farmers were traditionally paid with a small check and a jar of the product for the space. In 1963, Philip Morris, Inc., bought the company and unfortunately abandoned the signs.

45 Peanuts.

46 February or March, in the days before Ash Wednesday, which marks the beginning of Lent.

47 John England (1786–1848), the Roman Catholic bishop who was born in Cork, Ireland, and responsible for all Catholics in Georgia and the Carolinas from 1820 to 1842.

48 The Moravians, who were followers of John Hus. Organized by Count Nicholas von Zinzendorf into the Unity of Brethren, they practiced communal management of economic, family, and religious life.

49 The Arkansas Traveler is the name of a tune, a play, and a quilt pattern, all taken from a classic folk story in which a traveler on horseback has become lost and approaches a fiddling squatter. The traveler becomes a straight man to the squatter's comic test of wits and eventually befriends the squatter by playing on his fiddle.

50 Pleasant Hill, Kentucky, founded in 1805, and South Union, Kentucky, founded soon thereafter. They were well-operated, successful utopian agrarian communities until the Civil War, when they suffered irreparable physical and financial damage. They closed in 1910 and 1922 respectively, but Pleasant Hill has been restored and is open for public tours.

51 In 1728 William Byrd II headed a commission to establish the boundary between North Carolina and Virginia. His *History of the Dividing Line* described places, events, and people he encountered while surveying the area, including graphic accounts of backwoods folks he dubbed "lubbers." Byrd considered these folks unhealthy, lazy, poor, ignorant, and unskilled – prototypical "poor white trash."

52 Smithfield, Virginia, where the process of curing takes from six months to two or more years.

53 Kappa Alpha Order, founded at Washington College (now Washington and Lee) in 1865. The men wear Confederate uniforms and their dates wear hoop skirts.

54 Heritage USA, in Fort Mill, South Carolina, opened in 1977 by Pentecostal television evangelists Jim and Tammy Faye Bakker.

55 John Henry, an African American hero who, according to tradition, worked on the Big Bend Tunnel of the C & O Railroad in West Virginia shortly after the Civil War. He lost his life in a steam-drilling contest.

56 Speaking in tongues. The belief in glossolalia as evidence of a profound ecstatic experience separated Pentecostals from others in the Holiness movement.

57 In Cajun country, a Sunday community dance.

58 Baptists and Methodists.

59 Birmingham, Alabama, the "Pittsburgh of the South," where iron and steel production made the city a major southern industrial center.

60 Coarse, sweet shreds of tobacco packed in foil pouches and used for chewing. Brand names include Beech Nut, Red Man, and Mail Pouch.

61 A term, often pejorative, for a southern textile worker.

62 Harvard.

63 The Creek Nation, a loose confederacy of tribes whose populations were the largest in the eastern half of the South.

64 In the eighteenth and nineteenth centuries, the tar, pitch, and turpentine industry was centered in North Carolina.

65 The Second Baptist Church in Baltimore. It was established in 1803.

66 Greeks. In 1905, five hundred Greek sponge divers arrived in Tarpon Springs after an enterprising sponge merchant discovered plentiful deepwater sponge there. They eventually established a thriving community with a Greek Orthodox church, restaurants, groceries, clubs, and other businesses.

67 The Highland Games and Gathering of Scottish Clans at Grandfather Mountain, North Carolina. In the eighteenth century, approximately 45,000 Highland Scots emigrated to the South. In 1790, the Scotch-Irish, many of whom came down the Great Wagon Road from Pennsylvania, constituted one-fifth to one-third of the white population in the South.

68 Krewes.

69 A Moon Pie. RC Cola was developed in 1933 in Columbus, Georgia, by successors to Claud Hatcher, a pharmacist who had first created a ginger ale called Royal Crown.

70 The base for gumbos and other Creole dishes. A roux is made by stirring flour very slowly while browning it in fat.

71 Hampden-Sydney College. Founded in southside Virginia in 1776, Hampden-Sydney is the country's tenth oldest institution of higher learning.

72 All these ingredients of traditional southern cooking were part of the Native American diet when Europeans arrived.

73 Thomas Merton (1915–68).

74 Vidalia, Georgia.

75 A mojo is a voodoo charm, sometimes a small sack containing objects that are thought to have magical properties or are associated with a person being hexed. It is used to cast or remove a spell.

76 To quote writer Larry Brown, "Treeing Walkers are coon hounds that have a lot of heart in a fight. Big dogs with long ears, they have markings of white with brown or black spots, long tails, and loud mouths. These dogs make champion coon hounds because of their ability to disregard a cold track in favor of a hot track. Scent gets old and loses its power. A Treeing Walker will pick up and run a coon track that's ten minutes old instead of a running one that's forty minutes old."

77 Huguenots, who came to colonial South Carolina from France following the revocation of the Edict of Nantes (1685). In 1700, they made up one-eighth of South Carolina's white population.

78 Muhammad Ali (b. 1942, as Cassius Clay) and Colonel Harland P. Sanders, the "colonel" of Kentucky Fried Chicken (1890–1980).

79 The watermelon, which has become a negative and positive cultural symbol of the South. Mark Twain wrote in *Pudd'nhead Wilson*, "The true southern watermelon is a boon apart and not to be mentioned with commoner things. It is chief of this world's luxuries, king by the Grace of God over all the fruits of the earth. When one has tasted it, he knows what the angels eat. It was not a southern watermelon that Eve took; we know it because she repented."

80 *River Road Recipes*, published by the Junior League of Baton Rouge. It was first published in 1959. At last count it was in its seventieth printing and had sold over 1.2 million copies. The group has also published *River Road Recipes II* (1976) and *River Road Recipes III* (1994).

81 Dixie beer, first brewed in 1907 by Valentine Merz.

82 Mississippi and West Virginia. In 1992, Mississippi's per capita income was $14,088, while West Virginia's was $15,065.

83 Hushpuppies. John Egerton provides this recipe in *Southern Food*:

> In a mixing bowl, combine 1 cup of self-rising white cornmeal, 1/2 cup of self-rising flour, 1/2 teaspoon of salt, and 1 teaspoon of sugar (or use regular meal and flour with the salt and sugar and add 1/2 teaspoon each of baking powder and baking soda). Blend 1 egg and add enough buttermilk to produce a thick batter that will drop slowly but easily from a teaspoon. To make golf-ball-sized pups, drop teaspoonfuls of batter into fat that is hot enough and deep enough for the morsel to float. Fry to a golden brown and drain on absorbent paper, keeping the cooked ones warm in a 150-degree oven until ready to serve with a platter of fish.

84 A puddinglike cornbread. Although the term was not used in print until 1906, food historians consider it to be most closely related to an Indian porridge called "suppone" or "suppawn." Here is a recipe for Indian pudding from *Thomas Jefferson's Cook Book*: "Chop fine 1/2 pound of suet. Mix with 1/2 cup of corn meal, 1 cup of molasses, 1/4 teaspoon of salt, and 1 quart of milk. Stir well and pour into baking dish. Set in a slow oven. As it bakes, add more milk to prevent it thickening and hardening. Two hours will bake it. It is eaten with butter and sugar, or molasses."

85 Charleston, South Carolina. The festival is named for its Italian birthplace and is usually held at the end of May.

86 J. Frank Norris (1877–1952), who from his pulpit and in his newspaper, *The Fundamentalist*, generated attacks on liberalism, especially as it manifested itself in his own denomination, the Southern Baptist Convention.

87 Redbones are solid red hound dogs, smaller than bluetick hounds and about the same size as Treeing Walkers. They are mainly used to hunt raccoons but may also be used for other game, like bobcats and cougars.

88 Robert Schuller, who operates out of Orange County, California. All of the others are from the South: Graham, North Carolina; Humbard, Arkansas; Falwell, Virginia; Robertson, Virginia; Swaggart, Louisiana; De Hann, Florida; and Kennedy, Florida.

89 Memphis, Tennessee, in the Lorraine Motel at 450 Mulberry Street, where Martin Luther King Jr. was assassinated in 1968.

90 In 1950, with the slogan, "Where men are men, trucks are Ford V8s." Ford dominated pickup sales for decades until other companies brought out trucks with cowboy names: Silverado, Sierra Classic, and Ram Chargers.

91 The United Daughters of the Confederacy, founded in Nashville.

92 Will Rogers (1879–1935).

93 Utica, Mississippi.

94 The maiden aunt. Maiden aunts were often dependent on the families of their brothers or sisters and became important as teachers, nurses, confidants, and disciplinarians within the family. Many stereotypical fictional examples exist, from Aunt Pittypat in *Gone with the Wind* to Sister in Eudora Welty's "Why I Live at the P.O."

95 David "Davy" Crockett (1786–1836).

96 Orange sections and grated coconut. Ambrosia is sometimes enhanced, or some would say ruined, by the addition of bananas, pecans, or little marshmallows.

97 Goo-Goo Clusters, a combination of caramel, marshmallow, peanuts, and pure milk chocolate, created in 1912 by William H. Campbell, in Nashville.

98 The two Marie Laveaus (1794–1881 and 1827–97).

99 "Charters," "BurGUNdy," "Carondelette," and "Frerette."

100 The Marquis de Lafayette (1757–1834). This major purchase of grits took place when he visited the United States in 1824–25.

101 Jack Daniel's sour mash whiskey – not to be confused with bourbon.

102 On Christmas Eve, "fires of joy" are burned all night along the Mississippi River from Baton Rouge to New Orleans.

103 Mark 16:17–18: "And these signs will accompany those who believe: in my name they will cast out demons; they will pick up serpents, and if they drink any deadly thing, it will not hurt them; they will lay their hands on the sick and they will recover."

104 Craig Claiborne (b. 1920), from Sunflower County, Mississippi.

105 Alabama, Florida, Georgia, Kentucky, Louisiana, Mississippi, North Carolina, South Carolina, and Texas.

106 In southern vernacular, "to fall over," as in, "Mr. Bubba's watermelon truck tumped over in the ditch."

107 Scuppernongs and muscadines.

108 First Family of Virginia.

109 The head, as in, "If you don't set that spit cup where somebody's not going to tump it over, I'm gonna hit you upside the head, boy."

110 Antoine's, established in 1840. They estimate that they have served over 3.5 million orders of the dish. They will not divulge the recipe to the public, but they *will* tell you that the sauce is a puree of a number of green vegetables other than spinach.

111 Galatoire's, which was established first in Birmingham, Alabama, in the 1880s. It moved into its present location, 209 Bourbon Street, in 1905.

112 Gaffney, South Carolina.

113 Greenville, Mississippi. Steaks and tamales are the specialties of the house.

114 A resident of New Orleans's Ninth Ward, where the accents are Brooklynesque, as in, "Where y'at"?

115 The small intestines of hogs, cooked in batter. In the poverty-stricken South, no part of a slaughtered animal was wasted. Craig Claiborne recommends that chitterlings always be served with vinegar, hot red pepper sauce, and finely chopped onion on the side.

116 The Piedmont Chatauqua, located at Salt Springs (now Lithia), Georgia. Brainchild of New South booster Henry W. Grady (1850–89), it featured an 8,000-seat tabernacle, two Italian Renaissance–style hotels, and a building for its summer college, which in its heyday attracted faculty from Yale, Harvard, Johns Hopkins, and the University of Virginia.

117 BC Powder, Stanback, or Goody's headache powder.

118 The mint julep, described as early as 1803 by John David, who noted its early morning consumption in his *Travels in the United States*. In other accounts the julep has been called "nectar to the Virginian, mother's milk to the Kentuckian and ambrosia to Southerners anywhere." Walker Percy followed "cud'n Walker's Uncle Will's Favorite Mint Julep Recipe":

> You need excellent Bourbon whiskey: rye or Scotch will not do. Put half an inch of sugar in the bottom of the glass and merely dampen it with water. Next, very quickly – and here is the trick in the procedure – crush your ice, actually powder it, preferably in a towel with a wooden mallet, so quickly that it remains dry, and, slipping two sprigs of fresh mint against the inside of the glass, cram the ice in right to the brim, packing it with your hand. Finally, fill the glass, which apparently has no room left for anything else, with bourbon, the older the better, and grate a bit of nutmeg on the top. The glass will frost immediately. Then settle back in your chair for half an hour of cumulative bliss."

119 William Franklin "Billy" Graham (b. 1918).

120 The University of Georgia.

121 Tennessee, Mississippi, Arkansas, Florida, and Oklahoma.

122 Sun Records Cafe, located at 706 Union Avenue in Memphis.

123 Boiled peanuts. They were considered a delicacy in the first thirty years after the Civil War, and neighborhood "peanut boilings" were a form of social intercourse in southern communities.

124 Acadians ('Cadians), who arrived in Louisiana beginning in 1765 after British forces drove them out of Canada. Within a generation, these exiles had so firmly reestablished themselves that they became the dominant culture in South Louisiana; they absorbed other ethnic groups, including the French Creoles (descendants of earlier French settlers), Spanish, Germans, and Anglo-Americans. The cross-cultural exchange between these groups produced a new Louisiana-based community – the Cajuns.

125 Voodoo, also called "vodun" and "hoodoo." It derives from the religion of Dahomey (present-day Benin) in West Africa, where the term "vodu" designates gods worshiped by Dahomeans. Voodoo is an underground American religious sect that has often merged with or borrowed from Christianity in its use of the crucifix and saints as religious symbols. The religion is widespread in many areas, and its adherents and practitioners are not limited to African Americans.

126 Both are made from 51 percent or more corn, but bourbon is always made from fresh corn, whereas sour mash contains some corn that has been allowed to sprout. Also, bourbon cannot be called bourbon unless it is produced in Kentucky.

127 Apple-cider vinegar, salt, and red pepper. As one moves west through the Deep South, barbecue sauces thicken and turn redder from a tomato or catsup base.

128 Mobile, Alabama.

129 Louisiana oysters.

130 Louisiana.

131 In the South Carolina low country. The name is associated with the seeds' African origin: they were first brought to the country by slaves in the seventeenth century. They are often used by South Carolina cooks in bread, cookies, and candy. Here's a recipe for benne seed wafers from John Egerton's *Southern Food*:

> Toast 2/3 cup of benne (sesame) seeds in a heavy pan in a preheated oven 400 degrees for about ten minutes, or until they take on a light brown color, and let cool. Cream together one stick of butter and one cup of light brown sugar. Add to the mixture one egg (beaten), 3/4 cup of all-purpose flour (sifted), and 1/4 teaspoon of baking powder, blending thoroughly. Next, add one teaspoon of vanilla extract and the 2/3 cup of toasted benne seeds. When the dough is well mixed, drop it by teaspoonfuls onto a buttered cookie sheet and bake in a preheated 325-degree oven for ten minutes. Let cookies cool for one minute and then remove to racks. They will harden and stick on sheet if

left longer. When completely cooled, store in tins with tight-fitting lids. The recipe will make about five dozen.

132 The Lumbee Indian tribe numbers more than 40,000 people in Robeson and neighboring counties in southeastern North Carolina.

133 Grillades. It is made with braised slices of veal or round steak. The meat is well-cooked with tomatoes and served with freshly cooked grits.

134 "Tacky" originated in the late-nineteenth-century South to describe a degenerate, useless horse. It also came to signify a poor white person, "hillbilly," or "cracker" of the southern states from Virginia to Georgia. It now means "shabby" or "vulgar."

135 Three: Mary Ann Mobley (1959), Lynda Meade (1960), and Susan Akin (1986).

136 St. Claude Street in the Ninth Ward, New Orleans.

137 At Moorhead, Mississippi. New Orleans writer Nancy Lemann claims that "if [Mississippi Deltans] go somewhere, to a strange place, they stand up on a table and yell out, 'Where does the Southern cross the Yellow Dog?' and then if someone yells out 'Moorehead' [*sic*] then they know they have a friend there."

138 Bill Neal (1950–91), owner of Crook's Corner and La Residence in Chapel Hill.

139 Pralines. The first pralines used almonds, but modern recipes usually call for pecans. Here is a recipe:

In a heavy iron pan, combine 2 cups sugar with 1 cup half-and-half cream and 1 tablespoon butter and bring to a boil.

In a separate heavy saucepan, melt 1/2 cup sugar until it is caramel color. Add the cream, butter, and sugar mixture to the caramel mixture. Add 2 cups pecan halves and cook to the soft-ball stage (235 degrees on candy thermometer). Remove from heat and beat until it thickens. Drop onto wax paper to harden. Yields 2 dozen pralines 2 1/2 to 3 inches in diameter.

140 When the stew was originally created in the early 1880s in Brunswick County, Virginia, squirrel was the main meat ingredient, although any game could be tossed in. Chicken is now usually substituted for squirrel. Other ingredients include onions, celery, green peppers, a ham bone (preferably from a Smithfield ham), tomatoes, potatoes, lima beans, corn, and seasonings.

141 Christian Broadcasting Network University, now called Regent University, founded in 1975 in Virginia Beach, Virginia.

142 A short-haired dog with specks. These dogs weigh from thirty-five to forty pounds and have sharp-pointed ears. Sometimes used for hunting, they are also well suited for catching hogs or for herding.

143 A jenny is a female mule. A henny is the offspring of a female mule and a stud horse.

144 Llana del Rio Cooperative Colony, a socialist community that practiced such reforms as an eight-hour work day, minimum wage, social security, and quality educational and cultural programs.

145 Phi Beta Sigma.

146 According to the *Oxford English Dictionary*, it means "something given over and above what is purchased, earned," or "to make good measure or by way of gratuity." In Louisiana parlance, it means "something extra."

147 "Touched by two Kings."

148 The late Neil Cargile (1929–95).

149 Very small.

150 An eastern North Carolina outlaw and Robin Hood–like bandit of the Civil War era. Lowrie was a Lumbee Indian. On March 3, 1865, he witnessed the execution of his father and brother. They had refused to serve the Confederacy as laborers, although they had been willing to fight as soldiers, and according to legend, they were forced to dig their own graves. In retaliation Lowrie subjected the white population of Robeson County, North Carolina, to a reign of terror that lasted a decade.

151 Cajun meats. *Andouille* is a smoked pork sausage, and *tasso* is a highly seasoned and smoked ham.

152 Ralph Reed (b. 1961).

153 Old Sparky is a three-legged oaken chair at the Florida State Penitentiary in which serial killer Ted Bundy was the 216th person to be executed. Yellow Mama is Alabama's state electric chair.

154 Charles Manson, imprisoned for life in California for masterminding the Tate-LaBianca murders in 1969. As a child, he lived in Kentucky with his grandparents.

155 Melungeons are dark-skinned people who have lived in the Appalachian Mountains since the 1790s. The greatest number of them live in Hancock County, Tennessee. They are probably a mixture of white, African American, and Native American blood, but their origins are mysterious. Various theories about melungeons maintain that they are descended from Phoenician sailors, a twelfth-century Welsh prince, survivors of Sir Walter Raleigh's lost settlement at Roanoke, Croatan and Cherokee Indians, or shipwrecked Portuguese sailors, from whom their name may have come. (In Portuguese, *melungo* means "shipmate.")

156 Hillary Clinton, who visited Bangladesh in the spring of 1995. Residents of a small community comprising members of the lowest Hindu caste were so impressed that they renamed their village "Hillarypara."

157 The Southern Baptist Convention, based in Atlanta. On June 20, 1995, a century and a half after its founding in Augusta, Georgia, the convention issued a resolution that included these statements:

> We lament and repudiate historic acts of evil such as slavery. . . .
>
> We genuinely repent of racism of which we have been guilty. We ask forgiveness from our African American brothers and sisters, acknowledging that our own healing is at stake.

The resolution was adopted overwhelmingly by the convention's 20,000 delegates.

158 A popular pink hair pomade.

159 School spankings. In a 1992 U.S. Education Department survey, Alabama reported 53,000 spankings, well behind Texas, which had 140,900.

160 Hog testicles. Joann Thomas of Lafayette County, Mississippi, recommends this preparation method: Boil them until the outer skin turns "kind of white." Then take them out and let them cool. Take a knife and slit each one down the side, peeling off the outer skin. Cut each testicle half-in-two. Take the little white vein out, and soak the testicles in salt water for about five minutes. Drain, then season with salt and pepper. Get the oil in your frying pan hot. Dredge the testicles lightly in flour and fry on low heat until they get a little color and are tender. They taste "a little like liver but better," reports Ms. Thomas, who has cooked them for sixty years.

161 Union Hill Cumberland Presbyterian Church in Athens, Alabama, charged hunters three dollars each to enter a coon-treeing contest and ten dollars to join the night hunt. Reverend Charles Hood said, "The coon hunt is a way to spread the word of God, to talk about Jesus Christ." Coonburgers were served before the treed coons were shot.

162 "MIZ-riz."

163 Half-in-two, as in the Robert Johnson song "Blues": "If she gets unruly, / thinks she don't wan do, / Take my 32-20, now, and cut her half-in-two."

164 The Museum of the Boy Scouts of America is in Murray, Ky.; the Country Doctor Museum, in Bailey, N.C.; the Warren Rifles Confederate Museum, in Front Royal, Va.; the Patent Model Museum, in Fort Smith, Ark.; the Schmidt Museum of Coca-Cola Memorabilia, in Elizabethtown, Ky.; and the Museum of Tobacco Art and History, in Nashville, Tenn.

165 Inadequate, sorry, broken-down, makeshift, not up to par. As in, "That is the most brokedick marching band I ever saw." In the noun form, one can also *be* a brokedick: "He's that old brokedick who stays over near Toccopola."

166 Juliette Gordon Low founded the Girl Scouts in Savannah, Georgia, in 1912. Today the organization serves 2.5 million girls, with the help of 800,000 adult volunteers.

167 Miss Mississippi, Cheryl Prewitt, who was Miss America in

1980. Following a car accident in 1968, Prewitt's left leg was shorter than her right. In 1974, at a revival meeting in Jackson, Mississippi, three hundred people joined in prayer over her left leg. "I was sitting there very calmly," she said. "We prayed and we asked. I sat and watched my leg grow out instantaneously two inches" (*New York Times*, September 10, 1979).

168 Shinola, a popular shoe polish.

169 The Volunteer Fire Department on Chincoteague Island, Virginia, sponsors an annual Pony Penning: in order to control the herd of wild ponies on neighboring Assateague Island, the horses are rounded up, forced to swim the channel between the two islands, and then auctioned off.

170 John Peterman, owner of the J. Peterman Company.

171 Depending on who you talk to, it can mean either a turtle or the female genitalia.

172 Collards, which Ayden celebrates with an annual festival. Horst kept the collards down just long enough to claim the prize.

173 A bottle of shook-up, warm Coca-Cola.

174 "Jesus Saves," "Christ [or Jesus] is the Answer," "Get Right with God," "Christ Died for Your Sins," and "Prepare to Meet Thy God."

175 Poke weed. The root is deadly and can kill you, as will too much of the berry's juice. The leaves, when boiled, make delicious poke salet. (The water they boil in should be drained off and refilled twice.)

176 The Tidewater, a region extending through the Chesapeake Bay of Virginia and Maryland and into northeastern North Carolina.

1 True. Leigh was born in Darjeeling, India, to British parents, and she spent her childhood in Europe.

2 Katharine Hepburn, Violet Venable, *Suddenly Last Summer*; Carroll Baker, Baby Doll, *Baby Doll*; Marlon Brando, Stanley Kowalski, *A Streetcar Named Desire*; Paul Newman, Brick, *Cat on a Hot Tin Roof*; Natalie Wood, Alva, *This Property Is Condemned*; Kirk Douglas, Tom, *Glass Menagerie*; Ed Begley, Boss Finley, *Sweet Bird of Youth*.

3 Florence Reece (1907–86), from Sharp's Chapel, Tennessee. When her husband was driven out of Harlan, Kentucky, she wrote the song to the tune of an old hymn, "I Am Going to Land on That Shore":

> If you go to Harlan County
> There is no neutral there.
> You will either be a union man
> Or a thug for J. H. Blair.
> Which side are you on?
> Which side are you on?

4 Jimmie Rodgers (1897–1933), a.k.a. the "Singing Brakeman." Rodgers composed such standards as "Peach Pickin' Time in Georgia" and "T for Texas."

5 McKinley Morganfield is known as Muddy Waters, Chester Burnett as Howlin' Wolf, and Ellas McDaniel (or Elias Bates) as Bo Diddley.

6 *When the Jack Hollers*, by Langston Hughes. *Porgy and Bess* was written by Charlestonian Dubose Heyward. *In Abraham's Bosom* was Paul Green's first success.

7 The Okefenokee Swamp. Pogo, Albert, and Porky were characters in Walt Kelly's comic strip *Pogo*, begun in 1946.

8 Bojangles. There is a nine-and-a-half-foot-tall aluminum statue of him at the corner of Adams and Leigh Streets in the Jackson Ward district of Richmond, where he was born. It is the only major monument in the city dedicated to someone who was born there.

9 New Orleans jazz trumpeter Louis Armstrong (1900–1971). He acquired the nickname in England from the editor of a music magazine.

10 The "Funky Chicken."

11 Riley B. "B. B." King (b. 1925), of Indianola, Mississippi.

12 *The Birth of a Nation*.

13 Shape-note singing. This name derives from the peculiar four-shape notation form used in *The Sacred Harp* and other singing-school books. The style was also called "fasola" singing, from the custom of singing the song through first using "fa-so-la" syllables before singing the words.

14 Blind Blake, Blind Willie McTell, Gary Davis, Blind Boy Fuller, and Blind Lemon Jefferson.

15 Bill Monroe (b. 1911). In 1938 Monroe formed the Blue Grass Boys, whose sound gave rise to the "bluegrass" style.

16 Lester Flatt (1914–79) and Earl Scruggs (b. 1924). Flatt and Scruggs occasionally appeared on the show as themselves.

17 Prissy, in *Gone with the Wind*. Prissy was played by the actress Thelma "Butterfly" McQueen.

18 The Wild Tchoupitoulas. Their album was released in 1976.

19 The Shag, which since the 1950s has been danced to the "beach music" of R&B bands. "Stay," by Maurice Williams and the Zodiacs, is a good example of beach music.

20 Roy Acuff (b. 1903), of Maynardville, Tennessee, who was elected in 1962.

21 Socialist Aunt Molly Jackson (1880–1960), who is known for writing over a hundred songs about the lives and struggles of Kentucky coal miners.

22 Jerry Lee Lewis (b. 1935).

23 The British in the Battle of New Orleans (1814), according to country singer Johnny Horton's 1950s hit.

24 WDIA. The station popularized Delta and Memphis blues music in the 1940s and 1950s, influencing the young Elvis Presley.

25 Abner Yokum, of *Li'l Abner*, by Al Capp, and Snuffy Smith, of *Barney Google*, by Billy DeBeck.

26 The plucked dulcimer, or Appalachian dulcimer.

27 XER (later XERA), established by Arkansan John R. Brinkley, the "goat-gland doctor," who promoted a cure for male sexual impotence that utilized the testicles of goats. XER was the first of several "X" stations that flourished during this period.

28 Virginia and North Carolina, respectively.

29 Buck dancing. Buck dancers, traditionally male, perform solo and informally, arms hanging loose and feet close to the floor.

30 Ted Turner (b. 1939), who owns Turner Broadcasting System as well as the Atlanta Braves and Atlanta Hawks.

31 "We Shall Overcome," which was adapted by Zilphia Horton, Frank Hamilton, Guy Carawan, and Pete Seeger. According to Carawan, the first use of the song in a mass protest may have been outside the mayor's office in Nashville in the early 1960s.

32 *Hush Hush . . . Sweet Charlotte.*

33 Bo and Luke Duke of *The Dukes of Hazzard.*

34 Buford Pusser (1937–74), who served as sheriff from 1964 to 1970, devoting his life to bringing law and order to a notoriously lawless area near the Mississippi state line. Pusser died in a suspicious car wreck in 1974. In Adamsville, Tennessee, one hundred miles east of Memphis, the Buford Pusser Festival is held annually in Buford Pusser Memorial Park. The Buford Pusser Museum at 342 Pusser Street is filled with Pusser memorabilia, like the size 13 1/2 shoes he was wearing when he died, his recliner, his high school yearbook, his slingshot, and scripts of the *Walking Tall* movies.

35 *Deliverance.* The 1970 James Dickey novel on which the movie is based does not include this bit of dialogue.

36 Billy Joe McCallister, in the 1967 pop song "Ode to Billy Joe," by Bobbie Gentry.

37 Otis Redding (1941–67), born in Dawson, Georgia.

38 False. In fact, Cash's total jail time, on a variety of minor charges, is less than thirty hours.

39 The Ryman Auditorium in Nashville. Built in 1892 by a riverboat captain, Ryman was the Opry's home from 1943 until the early 1970s.

40 *King Creole* (1958).

41 James Brown (b. 1928).

42 "Take My Hand, Precious Lord." The first stanza reads,

> Precious Lord, take my hand, lead me on, let me stand.
> I am tired, I am weak, I am worn.
> Through the storm, through the night, lead me on to the
>   light
> Take my hand, Precious Lord, lead me home.

43 Patsy Cline. Born in 1932, she died in a plane crash in 1963.

44 A square dance.

45 The Blackwood Brothers.

46 Louisiana Cajun music.

47 John Luther "Casey" Jones (1863–1900). On April 29, 1900, Jones was trying to make up ninety-five minutes on a run between Memphis and Canton, Mississippi, on a train called the Cannonball. In the foggy dark at Vaughan, the Cannonball rammed a stalled train, and Jones was killed.

48 Jelly Roll Morton (1885–1941).

49 Louis Gottschalk (1829–69).

50 *Kudzu*, introduced in 1981 by Doug Marlette, who was then at the *Charlotte Observer*.

51 Hattie McDaniel (1895–1952). Her performance earned her an Oscar for Best Supporting Actress.

52 *Norma Rae*. For her role as Norma Rae, a prounion textile worker, Sally Field received an Oscar for Best Actress.

53 Capricorn Records, which signed such definitive southern rock groups as the Allman Brothers and the Marshall Tucker Band and is still operating in Atlanta and Nashville.

54 Willie Nelson, Texas; Patsy Cline, Virginia; Roy Acuff, Tennessee; Bill Monroe, Kentucky; Charley Pride, Mississippi; Earl Scruggs, North Carolina.

55 Tallulah Bankhead, dahling (1902–68).

56 Leontyne Price (b. 1927).

57 The Grand Ole Opry, which began broadcasting in 1925 as a series of Saturday night "barn dances." WSM program director George Hay gave it the name "Grand Ole Opry" in 1927.

58 Hank Williams (1923–53).

59 Dolly Parton (b. 1946). Her show started in 1976.

60 Mary Ann Mobley (b. 1939).

61 *The Real McCoys.*

62 Lester Young, tenor saxophone; King Oliver, cornet; Jelly Roll Morton, piano; Pete Fountain, clarinet; Louis Armstrong, trumpet.

63 William Christopher ("W. C.") Handy (1873–1958), born in Florence, Alabama.

64 "Strange Fruit." Writer Lillian Smith later borrowed this title for her controversial 1944 book about an interracial affair.

65 "Amazing Grace," written by John Newton (1725–1807), who gave up his life at sea to become a minister. The song is sung to different tunes, but its most familiar form is the one that appears in the shape-note tunebook *The Southern Harmony* (1835). Here are the first three verses:

> Amazing grace! how sweet the sound,
> That saved a wretch like me!
> I once was lost, but now I'm found,
> Was blind but now I see.

> 'Twas grace that taught my heart to fear,
> And grace my fears relieved;
> How precious did that grace appear
> The hour I first believed.

> Thro' many dangers, toils and snares,
> I have already come;
> 'Tis grace has brought me safe thus far,
> And grace will lead me home.

66 "Dixie's Land." It was first sung by Bryant's Minstrels at Mechanics Hall in New York City on April 4, 1859. After the tune was adopted as the war anthem of the Confederacy, Emmett composed new lyrics for the melody, urging Union troops to "meet southern traitors with iron." In the motion picture *Dixie* (1943), the song's story was dramatized, and Bing Crosby played Emmett.

67 Burt Reynolds (b. 1936).

68 "Go Down, Moses." First printed in 1872, the song had twenty-five verses, of which this is the first and the refrain:

> Go down, Moses,
> Way down in Egypt land,
> Tell ole Pharaoh
> To let my people go.

69 Highway 61, which parallels the Mississippi River from New Orleans to the Canadian border. Dylan's song "Highway 61" was written in 1965.

70 *Appalachian Spring*.

71 The Mississippi State Penitentiary at Parchman, in the Mississippi Delta.

72 A hellhound. "Hellhound on My Trail" was recorded in 1937 at what would be Johnson's last recording session.

73 Lewis Grizzard (1946–94), well-known humor columnist for the *Atlanta Constitution*.

74 The Great Smokies, near the junction of the Carolinas, Georgia, and Tennessee. The Smokies range, which includes some eighty peaks over 5,000 feet high, is about 140 miles long and 70 miles wide. The song is "On Top of Old Smoky."

75 *The City of New Orleans*, which still makes regular runs between Chicago and New Orleans.

76 Zydeco. The style is an accurate reflection of Louisiana's multicultural heritage. A vest *frottoir* is a metal rubbing board worn on one's chest and played with spoons, can openers, or thimbles.

77 Aaron Neville (b. 1941).

78 Albert Brumley (1905–77). The song has been recorded over five hundred times since its publication in 1932.

79 Hunter S. Thompson (b. 1937).

80 Proto-banjos made from gourds were brought to America by slaves from Africa.

81 Jimmy Buffett, who attended the University of Southern Mississippi in Hattiesburg, a far cry from Margaritaville. Buffett's song "Cheeseburger in Paradise" was a 1978 hit.

82 *The Color Purple*, which was directed by Steven Spielberg and grossed $29 million during its first month of release. The book also won a Pulitzer Prize and an American Book Award.

83 Misty was a pony from Chincoteague, Virginia. Like the other ponies on this Eastern Shore island, she was supposedly descended from horses who swam ashore from a capsized Spanish ship in the seventeenth century. The book by Marguerite Henry and a 1961 movie, both titled *Misty of Chincoteague*, are based on Misty's life with the Beebe family. You can still visit Misty at the Miniature Pony Farm in Chincoteague, where she has been preserved.

84 James Taylor (b. 1948).

85 Allman Brothers, Macon, Ga.; Marshall Tucker Band, Spartanburg, S.C.; Lynyrd Skynyrd, Jacksonville, Fla.; Charlie Daniels Band, Nashville; Amazing Rhythm Aces, Memphis.

86 *Hee-Haw*, hosted by Roy Clark and Alvis Edgar "Buck" Owens until Owens left the show in 1986. The show's bad jokes were delivered, appropriately enough, from a cornfield.

87 *Smokey and the Bandit*, starring Burt Reynolds, Sally Field, Jerry Reed, and Jackie Gleason. In 1977 it yielded $39,744,000, ranking it third in movie sales for that year.

88 Little Richard (b. 1935), born Richard Penniman.

89 A rockabilly version of Bill Monroe's "Blue Moon of Kentucky."

90 The recording was made in July 1976 at the Fox Theater, located on Peachtree Street across from the Georgian Terrace Hotel, where the movie *Gone with the Wind* premiered in 1939. It is said that you can practically hear the cigarette lighters. The recording is on the album *One More from the Road*.

91 "Love in Vain" and "Crossroads," respectively. Johnson had recorded those songs at the last session of his life, in June 1937. "Love in Vain" was, to Keith Richards, "such a beautiful song. Mick and I both loved it. . . . It was like, we've got to do this song one way or another." Of Johnson, Eric Clapton has said, "His music remains the most powerful cry that I think you can find in the human voice, really."

92 Johnny Cash (b. 1932).

93 Guitarist Johnny Winter (b. 1944), who is also partially blind.

94 Kim Basinger, who grew up in Athens, Georgia, purchased Braselton, Georgia, in 1989 for $20 million.

95 *Designing Women.*

96 Bessie Smith (1894–1937).

97 Wendell Scott.

98 South of the Border, off I-95 in Dillon, South Carolina. The complex features three hundred rooms, six restaurants, an amusement park, a miniature golf course, campgrounds, a lounge, and two pools.

99 Clifton Chenier (1925–88) of south Louisiana.

100 "Will the Circle Be Unbroken." The song was first recorded in 1935 by the Carter Family of Clinch Mountain, Virginia. The group comprised A. P. Carter; his wife, Sara; and his sister-in-law, Maybelle.

101 Athens, where a very fertile music scene developed in the 1980s.

102 Muscle Shoals, where the superior and funky studio musicians attracted many of the world's best R&B and rock groups.

103 Katie Couric (b. 1957).

104 Patsy Cline, "The Big Bopper," Otis Redding, the Barkays, and some members of the group Lynyrd Skynyrd.

105 Alex Chilton (b. 1950).

106 The Bubba Gump Shrimp Company, named for Forrest's Vietnam buddy, Benjamin Buford "Bubba" Blue of Bayou La-Batre, Alabama.

107 *Nashville*, appropriately enough.

108 Sissy Hankshaw.

109 Hank Williams Jr. (b. 1949), so nicknamed by his daddy, in honor of a puppet on the Grand Ole Opry.

110 Allman Brothers Band member Duane Allman was killed in 1971 on the corner of Log Cabin Drive and Hillcrest near Macon, and bass player Berry Oakley died nearby in 1972.

111 On Tuesday, December 4, 1956, Elvis Presley joined Carl Perkins at the end of Perkins's recording session at Sun Records in Memphis. Sun's founder, Sam Phillips, had recently acquired pianist Jerry Lee Lewis, who two weeks earlier had cut his first record. Phillips phoned Johnny Cash, who was in Memphis working on his fifth single. Cash came to the studio and joined the others on *Blueberry Hill* and *Isle of Golden Dreams*, recordings which have never been found. Approximately forty-one other cuts, mostly country, gospel, and R&B, plus studio chatter by Presley, Perkins, and Lewis, are available on an RCA/BMG compact disc.

112 Stagger Lee. Price's hit was released in 1959.

113 Brenda Mae Tarpley, a.k.a. Brenda Lee, of Atlanta, Georgia.

114 "Georgia on My Mind" (1960).

115 His mother-in-law. K-Doe's song "Mother-in-Law" hit number one on the charts in 1961.

116 On New Year's Eve, 1913, he was arrested for firing his father's .38 pistol. He was sent to the New Orleans Waif's Home for Boys, where the music teacher took an interest in him.

117 The Statler Brothers, who have recorded more than forty albums and are still together. They were originally called the Kingsmen.

118 W. C. Handy, born in Florence, Ala., in 1873. Hooker was born in Clarksdale, Miss.; King in Indianola, Miss.; and Waters in Rolling Fork, Miss.

119 Wolfman Jack (1938–95), whose real name was Robert Smith. He had just concluded a promotional tour for his book *Have Mercy* when he died. In 1973, he played himself in the movie *American Graffiti*.

120 Southern Made Doughnuts.

121 Samuel L. Jackson (b. 1949), who played Jules in *Pulp Fiction* (1994).

122 Squirrel Nut Zippers, a retro-jazz band.

123 The original Ronald McDonald, created and played by Willard Scott, a native of Alexandria, Virginia. When the Ronald McDonald character went national in 1965, the McDonald corporation gave the role to Coco, a Ringling Brothers clown, because it felt that Scott was too obese for the "active" image they wanted to convey. When asked how he felt about the company's decision, Scott, now a weatherman at NBC, replied, "Getting the part meant a lot to me then, and it was a total disappointment. It was the first time I was really screwed by the mass media."

124 Yul Brynner. Joanne Woodward played his niece, Quentin – Caddy's illegitimate daughter.

125 In 1918, convicted of murder and assault to murder, he was sentenced to thirty years' hard labor at the Central State Farm near Houston, Texas. He sang songs to help make the difficult work less onerous. The prison chaplain, observing Ledbetter's industriousness, remarked, "You're a hard-driving man. Instead of guts, you've got lead in your belly. That's who you are, old Leadbelly!" When Texas governor Pat M. Neff visited Ledbetter in prison, Ledbetter sang him a plea of mercy: "[If I had] you, Governor Neff, like you got me, / I'd wake up in the mornin' and I'd set you free." Ledbetter was pardoned by Governor Neff in 1925.

126 Colonel Tom Parker (b. 1909), a native of The Netherlands.

127 Link, Vernon, and Doug Wray, whose music has been described as "a cross between rockabilly and scary surf instrumentals by guys who not only didn't surf but never came out in the daylight."

LITERATURE

1 *Mandingo*, by Kyle Onstott. The novel was wildly inaccurate from a historical perspective.

2 Blanche DuBois, in Tennessee Williams's *A Streetcar Named Desire*.

3 Brer Rabbit, as recorded in *Nights with Uncle Remus* (c. 1881), by Joel Chandler Harris (1848–1908).

4 *Let Us Now Praise Famous Men*, by James Agee, with photographs by Walker Evans. The project was originally commissioned as an article for *Fortune* magazine.

5 The *Foxfire* books, which were taken from the *Foxfire* magazine, a project developed by ninth- and tenth-grade English teacher B. Eliot Wigginton and his students. The magazine and books featured topics ranging from crafts to folk remedies to mule swapping. With an initial investment of $440, the first book in the series (published in 1972) sold some three million copies.

6 The Agrarians, who in the late 1920s and early 1930s grew out of the Vanderbilt literary circle that was known as the Fugitives. In 1930 the Agrarians published *I'll Take My Stand*, their defense of the traditional southern agrarian culture against modern industrial society.

7 Richard Wright (1908–60), who wrote four stories that were published as *Uncle Tom's Children* (1938), and Eudora Welty (b. 1909), who traveled and wrote for the project's Mississippi guidebook.

8 Frederick Douglass (1808–95), whose *Narrative of the Life of Frederick Douglass: An American Slave* was published in 1845.

9 Ernest Gaines (b. 1933), born in Oscar, Louisiana. Since 1982 Gaines has been professor of English and writer in residence at the University of Southwestern Louisiana.

10 *All God's Dangers*, the powerful recollections of Ned Cobb (Nate Shaw) (1885–1973), as told to Theodore Rosengarten.

11 *Brother to a Dragonfly* (1977).

12 Frank Yerby (b. 1916).

13 Jean Toomer (1894–1967).

14 The *Sewanee Review*, published at the University of the South, in Sewanee, Tennessee, since 1892.

15 *End as a Man* (1947), by Calder Willingham, and *Lords of Discipline* (1980), by Pat Conroy.

16 Margaret Mitchell (1900–1949), who wrote *Gone with the Wind* (1936).

17 Wilbur Joseph Cash (1900–1941).

18 Kate Chopin, Flannery O'Connor, Walker and William Alexander Percy, Katherine Anne Porter, and Allen Tate.

19 The Sears, Roebuck catalog, which is no longer published.

20 *Strange Fruit*, by Lillian Smith (1897–1966), one of the most outspoken southern liberals during the 1930s and 1940s. The book was translated into fifteen languages, banned in Boston, and produced as a Broadway play.

21 Willie Stark, in Robert Penn Warren's Pulitzer Prize–winning novel *All the King's Men* (1946). Willie Stark was based on Huey Long, legendary governor and senator from Louisiana.

22 *Uncle Tom's Cabin* (1853), by Harriet Beecher Stowe.

23 Joseph Glover Baldwin (1815–64). His popular book *The Flush Times of Alabama and Mississippi* was published in 1853.

24 George Moses Horton (1797–1883?), one of ten children born to a slave in Northampton County, North Carolina. While selling produce in Chapel Hill, Horton recited his original poems, and in 1829 students published twenty-one of them (*The Hope of Liberty*) to finance his trip to Liberia. Later collections of Horton's poetry were published in 1845 and 1865.

25 James Agee (1909–55), who spent his early life in Knoxville. Agee is best known for the classic *Let Us Now Praise Famous Men*, his collaboration with photographer Walker Evans.

26 *The Dollmaker* (1954). This book was the basis for the 1984 film of the same name, starring Jane Fonda.

27 *The Sot-weed Factor* (1960), a darkly comic tale. Cooke's 1708 poem of the same name was a satirical commentary on life in early Maryland.

28 Ignatius J. Reilly in *A Confederacy of Dunces*, a hilarious novel by John Kennedy Toole (1937–69). Reilly was described as a "slob extraordinary, a mad Oliver Hardy, a fat Don Quixote, a perverse Thomas Aquinas, who is in revolt against the entire modern age." Toole committed suicide in 1969, and his mother took the manuscript to Walker Percy, who arranged for its publication.

29 James Dickey (b. 1923), of Columbia, South Carolina.

30 Margaret Walker Alexander (b. 1915), of Jackson, Mississippi.

31 "Song of the Chattahoochee," by Sidney Lanier (1842–81), the South's finest poet in the years just after the Civil War.

32 Tennessee Williams (1912–83).

33 Sister, who tells her story in Eudora Welty's "Why I Live at the P.O.," a story first published in the *Atlantic Monthly* in 1941.

34 Carson McCullers (1917–67). Her 1940 novel was *The Heart Is a Lonely Hunter*.

35 Charles Dickens (1812–70), who described the meeting in *American Notes and Pictures from Italy*.

36 Shelby Foote (b. 1916), who took twenty years to write *The Civil War: A Narrative* (1974).

37 William Byrd II (1674–1744), of Westover. Byrd was a lawyer, planter, businessman, and member of the Royal Society and the Virginia House of Burgesses.

38 On Tobacco Road, near Augusta, Georgia. *Tobacco Road*, first published in 1932, has sold over three and a half million copies, has been translated into fifteen languages, and was made into a movie and a Broadway play with a seven-year run.

39 Wendell Berry (b. 1934). Berry has won Guggenheim and Rockefeller Foundation fellowships and an award from the American Academy and Institute of Art and Letters.

40 *The Oldest Living Confederate Widow Tells All*, by Allan Gurganus. Marsden tells an interviewer, "Why honey, I'm a veteran of the veteran."

41 Allen Tate (1899–1979), who wrote "Ode to the Confederate Dead," and Henry Timrod (1828–67), who wrote "Ode," which was read "on the Occasion of Decorating the Graves of Confederate Dead at Magnolia Cemetery." A few lines from Timrod's poem go like this:

Sleep sweetly in your humble graves,
Sleep, martyrs of a fallen cause!
Though yet no marble column craves
The pilgrim here to pause.

42 John Peale Bishop (1892–1944), born in Charles Town, West Virginia.

43 Cleanth Brooks (1906–93), who was also a Rhodes Scholar, twice a Guggenheim Fellow, cultural attaché to England, and author and editor of many books that have shaped the way we read and understand literature today.

44 Miss Daisy. *Driving Miss Daisy* was written by Alfred Uhry.

45 George Webber, in Thomas Wolfe's novel *You Can't Go Home Again* (1940). Home was Libya Hill, which, like Altamont of *Look Homeward, Angel* (1929), was modeled on Wolfe's native Asheville, North Carolina.

46 Willie Morris (b. 1934), a native of Yazoo City, Mississippi, who published his candid autobiography *North Toward Home* in 1967. Morris now resides in Jackson, Mississippi; his book *New York Days* (1993) is about the *Harper's* years.

47 Frances Hodgson Burnett (1849–1924), whose most popular work was probably *The Secret Garden* (1911). Burnett had to pick grapes to earn enough money for the paper, ink, and stamps to publish her first story.

48 *Invisible Man* (1952), by Ralph Ellison.

49 Harper Lee (b. 1926) based Dill on her childhood friend Truman Streckfus Persons, a.k.a. Truman Capote, whom she had known in Monroeville, Alabama, where Capote had lived with relatives. John Megna, the actor who played Dill in the 1942 movie version of the book, died of AIDS in September 1995 at the age of 42.

50 *The Habit of Being*.

51 The University of Mississippi.

52 William Faulkner's Snopeses.

53 Harry Crews (b. 1935).

54 Stingo is the Virginian protagonist and narrator of William Styron's 1979 novel, *Sophie's Choice*. Stingo was in love with the tragic Sophie.

55 Peter Taylor (1917–94), who published *Happy Families Are All Alike* (1959), *In the Miro District* (1977), and *In the Tennessee Country* (1994), among others.

56 James Branch Cabell (1879–1958). *Jurgen* caused the publisher to be charged with violating New York's pornography laws, but it was exonerated and became a milestone in the treatment of sex in American literature.

57 *Roots*, by Alex Haley.

58 *Upper Room*, *Southern Living*, *Boy's Life*, and *Mother Earth News*.

59 Fanny Kemble (1809–93), who published *Journal of a Residence in America* (1835) and *Journal of a Residence on a Georgian Plantation* (1863). The latter was meant to influence British opinion during the Civil War.

60 Tom Wolfe (b. 1931) of Richmond, Virginia.

61 Pearl Buck (1892–1973), author of *The Good Earth*. This novel and many other Buck novels are set in China, where she spent most of her childhood years with her missionary parents.

62 Maya Angelou (b. 1928). The poem was called "On the Pulse of Morning."

63 Deacon Lunchbox, a.k.a. Tim Ruttenber (1951–92), was the poet laureate of Ponce de Leon Avenue in Atlanta. He described himself as a "socially conscious redneck poet using backwoods southern imagery to espouse a progressive political stance, like a redneck Tom Waits." For example:

> They got dope-sniffin' dogs at Dollywood
> My vacation plans are ruined
> The anti-drug hysteria is overdone
> The more I hear about crack
> The more I want to try some.

64 John Grisham (b. 1955), who practiced law in Southhaven, Mississippi, until his second novel, *The Firm* (1991), was optioned for $600,000 by Paramount while still in manuscript. More than 55 million copies of his books are in print, and three have been turned into box office hits.

65 Marjorie Kinnan Rawlings (1896–1953), who was best known for her novel *The Yearling* (1938), a coming-of-age story about a boy and his backcountry family.

66 Oxford, Mississippi, which at various times has been the home of writers William Faulkner, John Faulkner, Stark Young, Willie Morris, Donna Tartt, Richard Ford, Ellen Douglas, Dean and Larry Wells, John Grisham, Barry Hannah, and Larry Brown.

67 In a gay bar called the Pickup, on Congress Street in Savannah, Georgia, according to John Berendt's best-selling book *Midnight in the Garden of Good and Evil* (1994). The book features numerous other unusual characters, such as Emma Kelly, "Lady of 6,000 Songs"; Jim Williams, an antique dealer who was tried four times for shooting and killing Danny Hansford, a Camaro-driving handyman; and Joe Odum, a piano-playing attorney who opens his home to daily luncheon tours for extra income.

68 They are the names and noms de plume of the same person, vampire novelist Anne Rice (b. 1941). Born Howard Allen O'Brien, she changed her first name in 1947 and married Stan Rice in 1961. Rice writes soft-porn romances under the pseudonym Anne Rampling and erotic sadomasochistic fantasies as A. N. Roquelaure.

69 William Faulkner. In his controversial 1931 novel *Sanctuary*, Popeye uses a corncob to rape Temple Drake.

70 Harper Lee: Scout Finch; William Styron: Stingo; Thomas Wolfe: Eugene Gant; Walker Percy: Will Barrett; Robert Penn Warren: Jack Burden; Richard Wright: Richard.

71 Zora Neale Hurston (1901–60).

SCIENCE, MEDICINE, BUSINESS, AND INDUSTRY

1 Arguably, air-conditioning. As early as the 1830s, Dr. John Gorrie (1803–55) began experimenting with mechanical cooling in an attempt to lower the body temperature of malaria and yellow fever victims. The first true air-conditioner was not invented until 1902, and the region's first air-conditioning system was installed at the Chronicle Cotton Mills in Belmont, North Carolina, in 1906. Gorrie's research on refrigerants also led to the creation of the first ice machine, perfected in 1847. You can find out more about this "cool" southern inventor at the John Gorrie State Museum in Apalachicola, Florida.

2 Peanuts may have arrived in the South on slave vessels, where they were used as food for slaves. The Congo word for peanut is *nguba*.

3 Delta Airlines. Today one of the most consistently profitable airlines in the country, Delta began as Huff Daland Dusters and first carried passengers from Monroe, Louisiana, in 1929.

4 Houston, Texas, founded in 1836 by two brothers from New York, John and Augustus Allen.

5 Tulane University, which began as the Medical College of Louisiana at New Orleans.

6 Holiday Inns.

7 Disease. The early European explorers brought epidemics of smallpox, diphtheria, scarlet fever, measles, yellow fever, and malaria that helped destroy Mississippian period culture.

8 On the Biltmore Estate in Asheville, North Carolina, in 1898. It was founded by George Vanderbilt's forester, Gifford Pinchot.

9 The cotton gin, invented by Eli Whitney to separate the seeds from the fibers.

10 Yellow fever. Following the New Orleans epidemic of 1905, the disease was brought under control after the discovery of its transmission by mosquitoes, understanding of gene theory, and other medical advances.

11 Carville, Louisiana. It was formerly a state institution but became national in the 1920s.

12 Artificial limbs.

13 Pellagra, which results from a deficiency of niacin, one of the B vitamins. Symptoms include lassitude, weakness, and irritability. By one estimate, in 1915 there were 25,000 cases of this disease in the South.

14 Rice, which was first planted in tidal marshes and soon cultivated along inland river marshes.

15 Corn, tobacco, rice, and indigo.

16 Thomas Jefferson's *Notes on the State of Virginia* (1786). Jefferson claimed that blacks were less beautiful than whites and their emotions less complex, and he compared them unfavorably with Roman slaves.

17 Cholera.

18 The Georgia and Florida; the Carolina and Northwestern; and the Houston, East and West Texas.

19 Anniston.

20 Georgia (72.2 years), Mississippi (72.0), South Carolina (71.8), and Louisiana (71.7).

21 The spittoon.

22 The Tuskegee Syphilis Experiment, in which over four hundred African American men were denied treatment for syphilis to compare the effects of the disease on blacks and whites. In 1974, the federal government agreed to pay the victims $10 million, although the scientists involved made no public apology.

23 Mary Breckinridge (1881–1965), who was born into a prominent southern family and educated at finishing schools in Switzerland and Connecticut. Imbued with her family's sense of noblesse oblige, she devoted her life to child welfare, bringing the concept of the professional nurse-midwife to the United States from England. In 1980, after fifty-five years of operation, the Frontier Nursing Service had supervised 18,885 maternity cases and lost only eleven mothers.

24 George Washington Carver (1864–1943). All his life, Carver endeavored to improve the conditions of poor and often landless black farmers in the South.

25 The Kentucky School for the Deaf and Mute, which opened in 1822.

26 With the help of his friend and publisher James D. B. DeBow, Alabama physician Josiah C. Nott (1804–73) argued in *Types of Mankind* that races were fixed types "permanent through all recorded time."

27 "John the Conqueror" root, or "High John the Conqueror" (*Hypericum punctatum*). The root grows wild, and its spotted leaves symbolize the blood of John the Baptist. Muddy Waters mentions it in a 1954 recording of his "Hootchie Kootchie Man."

28 False. In 1860, the value of the combined crops of hay and cereals grown in the South exceeded that of cotton by over $900 million. What made cotton king was its easy negotiability and its attractiveness in the world market. Corn, in contrast, was little traded beyond the locale in which it was grown.

29 Brown lung disease, or "Monday fever," which is caused by exposure to cotton dust. Before the Occupational Safety and Health Administration (OSHA) enacted regulations for cotton dust exposure, many southern textile workers were afflicted with the disease.

30 Charles Alderton, of Waco, Texas, created the drink in 1885 and named it for Dr. Charles K. Pepper of Rural Retreat, Virginia.

31 The Baltimore and Ohio, established in the 1830s.

32 Ephraim McDowell (1771–1830).

33 Federal Express, created in 1973, which now serves 185 countries and delivers to virtually every location in America.

34 Gatorade. It was developed in 1965 by Dr. Robert Cade.

35 Black lung disease, which in the mid-1960s afflicted one in ten working miners, and one in five nonworking miners, in the bituminous coal mines of Appalachia. In 1968, 40,000 miners went on strike over the refusal of the West Virginia legislature to make the disease compensable. The Coal Mine Health and Safety Act of 1969 finally provided mandatory industry guidelines and compensation for the families of black lung victims.

36 The right one, Pepsi-Cola. Uh-huh.

37 Samuel P. Moore (1813–89), who ran what is generally regarded as one of the most efficient departments in the Confederacy.

38 Walter Reed (1851–1902), born near Gloucester, Virginia. He also investigated and helped eradicate typhoid and malaria, two other diseases that plagued the South.

39 James B. Duke (1856–1925). He organized the tobacco business begun by his father into the American Tobacco Company, established Duke Power Company, and in 1892 brought Trinity College to Durham and renamed it Duke University.

40 Maxwell House, created by Joel O. Cheek.

41 Soybeans.

42 Electricity.

43 Entrepreneur Henry Flagler (1830–1913). Perhaps his greatest contribution was developing a railroad system, which transported visitors in and produce out.

44 Tabasco sauce, made by the McIlhenny family since 1868. It is also an ingredient in a reliable southern hangover cure. The cure (not advertised by the company) is a concoction of raw egg, Tabasco, and Lea and Perrins Worcestershire sauce.

45 The Delta Queen, which has been plying the Mississippi since 1890.

46 Dirt-eating, which is a common practice among some southern women, especially some African Americans, in whom it was first observed during slavery. The practice was spread north by the black migration. Urban northerners often continue the practice by substituting laundry starch.

47 The red imported fire ant (*Solenopsis invicta*), which arrived in wood off a freighter in Mobile about seventy years ago.

48 North Carolina.

49 Coca-Cola, concocted in 1886 by John S. "Doc" Pemberton of Atlanta. In 1898, Pemberton grossed a whopping $50 in sales of his new beverage. The original recipe included minute amounts of cocaine, which were removed in 1905 due to public concern. It is now sold in approximately 195 countries and advertised in eighty languages.

50 Piggly Wiggly.

51 South Carolina. Wadmalah Island, near Charleston, is home to the Charleston Tea Plantation, where American Classic Tea is produced. Over one hundred years ago, tea planters brought specimens from China, India, and Ceylon. The tea plants cultivated today are descendants of those originals.

52 Hadacol (pronounced "HADDY-col") was the patent medicine sold by the Cajun state senator "Coozan" Dudley LeBlanc of Louisiana in the early 1950s. This mixture of B vitamins and alcohol was reputed to be an aphrodisiac as well as a cure for various ills. LeBlanc's Hadacol Traveling Show, which barnstormed the South, included such stars as Chico Marx, Bob Hope, Cesar Romero, Hank Williams, and Minnie Pearl.

53 Wal-Mart, created by Sam Moore Walton (1918–92), of Bentonville, Arkansas. The heirs of the late Mr. Walton are the world's richest family, with a net worth of over $23 billion.

54 Texas and Florida. Eight of the top ten states were in the South.

55 RJR Nabisco, which is now headquartered in New York City and whose worldwide income in 1991 exceeded $15 billion.

56 Texas and California. Mississippi ranks third, followed by Arkansas and Louisiana.

57 North Carolina, which produced 609,873 pounds in 1991. It is followed by Kentucky, Tennessee, South Carolina, and Virginia.

58 The Port of South Louisiana, which handled 189,374,451 tons of goods in 1991. Of the top ten busiest ports in America, seven are in the South, and four are in Louisiana.

59 Kentucky Fried Chicken.

60 In 1919 the McCarty and Holman families opened the first Jitney in Jackson, Mississippi. Back then the slang word for "nickel" was "jitney," and the store's slogan was "Save a nickel on every quarter." According to legend, a misprint in a newspaper advertisement changed the store's name from Jitney *Jingle* to Jitney *Jungle*. But Eudora Welty says this about her neighborhood Jitney (Jitney #14): "I always felt it was named Jitney Jungle because it was like exploring to go into the aisles. . . . I feel the same way about Jitney #14 as I do about story writing. . . . Life goes on; . . . you can't live in the past and you must be aware of reality. You need to reflect change and progress with the times." Jitney Jungle has stores in Mississippi, Louisiana, Tennessee, Arkansas, Alabama, and Florida.

61 Leeches (*Hirudo medicinalis*), which release chemicals in their saliva that numb the skin, dilate the veins, and thin the blood, keeping clots from forming during reattachment surgery. Biopharm, a company based in Charleston, South Carolina, is the country's largest breeder of leeches used for this purpose.

62 The Cabbage Patch Dolls, which were supposedly conceived in a magic cabbage patch in the mountains of Georgia. They were actually designed by Georgia artist Xavier Roberts in 1976. Seventy-five million dolls were adopted during the ten-year Cabbage Patch craze.

63 0.

64 The Slater system was the model for the first American factories, developed in New England in the early 1800s. As adopted in the South, it employed whole families, including women and children, in contrast to the later Lowell system, which employed mostly immigrants and men.

65 Nashville, where these practices began during the Civil War.

66 At the U.S. Space and Rocket Center in Huntsville, Alabama. There are rides, movies, dozens of hands-on exhibits, and fifteen hundred artifacts, including rockets, space capsules, and missiles. Approximately 400,000 visitors come to the center every year.

67 Maker's Mark Distillery, located two miles east of Loretto, in the Bluegrass heartland of Kentucky.

68 Bowling Green, Kentucky.

69 Saturn, General Motors' first domestic car manufacturing division since Chevrolet debuted in 1911. Established in 1985, Saturn currently has 326 domestic retail facilities, plus seventy facilities in Canada and twenty in Taiwan. Saturn still farms the land around its Spring Hill plant and supports a Citizens' Environmental Council. In June 1995, the company hosted the Saturn Homecoming, which drew 44,000 Saturn enthusiasts to Spring Hill.

70 NUCOR Steel, in Charlotte, North Carolina. The company's first mill opened in Darlington, South Carolina, in 1968, and reported $11.5 million in sales in 1994.

71 Cracker Barrel Old Country Store, Inc., whose common stock is traded in the over-the-counter market under the NASDAQ symbol CBRL.

72 Northwest/KLM, which has a hub in Memphis, Tennessee.

73 Winston-Salem, North Carolina, where the Garner family has made sauce since 1929.

ART AND ARCHITECTURE

1 Black Mountain College. Josef Albers, Walter Gropius, Willem de Kooning, Buckminster Fuller, and Robert Motherwell were among those who taught there.

2 Mathew Brady (c. 1823–96).

3 John White (flourished 1585–93).

4 John Tyler (1790–1862). Sherwood Forest is unusual in that it is only one room deep yet stretches to three hundred feet in length because Tyler chose to enclose the exterior passageways to the flanking dependencies of the main house.

5 The John C. Campbell Folk School at Brasstown, North Carolina, which has assisted southern mountain people in preserving their culture since 1925.

6 John McCrady (1911–68).

7 Mt. Vernon, home of George Washington. She formed the Mt. Vernon Ladies Association of the Union, which still operates the property today.

8 Williamsburg, Virginia.

9 Thomas Sully (1783–1872).

10 Lewis Hine (1879–1940). He was hired for this work by the National Child Labor Committee.

11 Stratford Hall, in Westmoreland County, Virginia.

12 William Christenberry, who was born just north of Hale County in 1936, the same year that Evans and Agee were working on the book.

13 Newcomb College in New Orleans, founded in 1886.

14 Columns, or "colyums," as Flem Snopes called them.

15 Stone Mountain, Georgia, where an 825-foot dome rises 1,683 feet above sea level. Carved into its side is the world's largest sculpture: a memorial to the Confederacy composed of the mounted figures of Robert E. Lee, Jefferson Davis, and Thomas J. "Stonewall" Jackson, the "Lost Cause Trinity." This memorial, which is 90 feet high by 190 feet wide, was begun in 1915, but most of the work was done between 1964 and 1970 by Walter Hancock, George Weiblin, and Roy Faulkner.

16 Jefferson Davis (1808–89).

17 The Edgefield district of South Carolina, where, around 1820, potters began applying wood ash or lime to create a dark brown or greenish glaze.

18 The Charleston single house.

19 The University of Virginia, which opened its doors in 1819.

20 Louisville, Kentucky. The building was completed in 1985.

21 Frederick Law Olmsted (1822–1903). Perhaps best known as the designer of New York's Central Park, Olmsted traveled extensively in the South in the 1850s and described the region in a series of articles for the *New York Daily Times*. These became the basis for several books, notably *Journey in the Seaboard Slave States* (1856) and *A Journey in the Back Country* (1860).

22 Wrought iron.

23 Joshua Johnston (1765–1830).

24 Drayton Hall, located outside of Charleston, South Carolina. Built around 1740, it features an almost square plan, a double portico, classical details, and richly carved woodwork and plasterwork. It is owned by the National Trust for Historic Preservation and is open to the public.

25 Thomas Hart Benton (1889–1975).

26 Arlington, home of Robert E. Lee and Mary Ann Custis Lee. Federal troops occupied the house in 1861, and the government auctioned off and illegally bought Arlington and established a national cemetery on the grounds in 1864. In 1882, a son of the Lees won a Supreme Court case regarding ownership of the estate, but for a fair monetary settlement he conveyed the property to Congress.

27 Fay Jones (b. 1921), who designed the chapel in 1981.

28 Edgar Degas (1834–1917). He lived in his uncle's home near Tonti and Esplanade. His family was in the cotton business, and of their livelihood Degas said, "Nothing but cotton. . . . One lives for cotton and from cotton." The bustle of the cotton exchange office is captured in his exquisitely composed painting *Portraits in an Office: The Cotton Exchange* (1873), now in the Musée des Beaux Arts, Paris.

29 Seaside.

30 George Ohr (1857–1918). Now considered one of the greatest American potters, he created extraordinary distorted, obscene, and violently colored ceramic vessels.

31 Romare Bearden (1914–88).

32 A dogtrot.

33 James Oglethorpe. In 1733 he established the town with a plan based on symmetrical squares, gardens, and broad avenues.

34 The Hermitage. The estate is located outside of Nashville, Tennessee, and ironically, is included in the historic Trail of Tears route administered by the National Parks Service. Along this road, many Native Americans lost their lives as they were forced to leave their homeland and march to reservations in the Oklahoma Territory in 1838. Jackson strongly advocated the brutal policies against Native Americans, including their forced migration.

35 In the South Carolina low country: specifically, in Charleston, and in Mt. Pleasant along Route 17.

36 Painter Robert Rauschenberg (b. 1925) and singer Janis Joplin (1943–70).

37 The Museum of Early Southern Decorative Arts (MESDA), in Winston-Salem, North Carolina.

38 Thomas Jefferson designed the structure in 1785, basing it on the Maison Carrée, a Roman temple in Nîmes, France. It was the first classical revival building in America.

39 Howard Finster (b. 1906), of Summerville, Georgia, creator of the spectacular Paradise Garden and the World Folk Art Church. His paintings are futuristic, apocalyptic, and evangelical and feature scripture, personal ideology, patriotism, and pop imagery.

40 Bacon's Castle, which was built around 1665 in Surry County, Virginia, by Arthur Allen, a planter and merchant. It features curvilinear gables, projecting entrance and rear stair towers, molded brick watertable, and pediment doorway, and two towering chimneys with free-standing stacks mounted diagonally. It is named Bacon's Castle because rebel soldiers took refuge there in 1676 during Bacon's Rebellion, led by Nathaniel Bacon. It is now owned by the Association for the Preservation of Virginia Antiquities and is open to the public.

41 In lower Louisiana and the lower Mississippi River Valley.

42 Charleston, South Carolina, where such carvings are a tribute to the crop that supported many citizens in high style.

43 John Portman (b. 1924). His most famous work is the Peachtree Center in Atlanta. He also designed numerous other structures across the country and in foreign countries such as Malaysia and Hong Kong.

44 Charles Rogers "Red" Grooms (b. 1937), who saw Nashville, where he grew up, "as an urban place, 'the Athens of the South.'" "I thought the country was anticultural, and Nashville a metropolis," he has said. "I had lots of civic pride." Grooms's family was staunchly Southern Baptist, and he took Saturday art classes with a teacher who painted cubist interpretations of the Grand Ole Opry. Both undoubtedly influenced his work. Of his fascination with pop culture, Grooms has said, "I think vulgarity is kind of charming!!"

45 Florida. Cracker houses, most of which were built in the late nineteenth and early twentieth centuries, generally have high-pitched tin roofs and board-and-batten siding. They were either single- or double-room structures, dogtrots, or I-houses.

46 Houston, Texas. The event is the largest gathering for art cars in the world. In 1995, the "Carmadillo," a fifty-foot-long, aluminum-plated creation by sculptor Mark Bradford, won the People's and Judges' Choice awards out of 240 entries. St. Louis and Atlanta also sponsor artmobile festivals.

47 Jasper Johns (b. 1930), who was born in Augusta, Georgia, studied at the University of South Carolina, and kept a studio on Edisto Island.

48 The tire. Car and truck tires can be planted as is, painted, or carved and formed into decorative urns.

49 The bottle gourd, *Lagenaria vulgaris*. Gourds encourage the nesting of purple martins, which help control mosquitoes and garden-harming insects.

SPORTS AND RECREATION

1 Althea Gibson (b. 1927), from North Carolina. Gibson became internationally recognized when she won tennis titles in France, Great Britain, and Italy. In 1957, she was ranked the number-one woman player in the United States, and in that year and 1958, she won the women's singles and doubles events at Wimbledon.

2 Cockfighting. Outlawed in most areas, cockfights occur throughout the country, but a disproportionate number of fans are white males in the rural South. There are three cockfighting publications and a lobbying group, the United Gamefowl Breeders Association.

3 1947.

4 Choctaws.

5 The Preakness is held in Baltimore, Maryland, and the Kentucky Derby, of course, in Louisville, Kentucky.

6 Streaking.

7 Isaac Murphy.

8 Atlantan Robert Tyre "Bobby" Jones Jr. (1902–71), who also helped design the Augusta National Golf Course because "my native Southland, especially my own neighborhood, had very few, if any, golf courses of championship quality."

9 National Association for Stock Car Auto Racing, Inc. The group was formed in 1947 to standardize the rules and administration of racing.

10 Carolina blue. And if God were not a Tar Heel, this would not be so.

11 Roll.

12 The University of South Carolina's Fighting Gamecocks.

13 In Raleigh, North Carolina, in connection with a farmer's market and tobacco festival.

14 The largemouth bass.

15 Willie McCovey, Amos Otis, Satchel Paige, and Hank Aaron are all from Mobile.

16 Tyrus Raymond "Ty" Cobb (1886–1961), from Banks County, Georgia, the first nationally known player from the South, and arguably the greatest of all professional baseball players.

17 Dollywood, near Pigeon Forge, Tennessee, named for Dolly Parton; Twitty City, outside of Nashville, named for Conway Twitty; Loretta Lynn's Dude Ranch, in Hurricane Mills, Tennessee; and George Jones' Country Music Park, outside of Colmesneil, Tennessee.

18 Jay Hanna "Dizzy" Dean (1911–76), who was born in Lucas, Arkansas, and is buried in Wiggins, Mississippi. There is a Dizzy Dean Museum in Jackson, Mississippi.

19 The 1979 Daytona 500.

20 The Kentucky Derby, held at Churchill Downs in Louisville since 1875. The Derby was patterned after England's Epsom Derby.

21 The University of Richmond's mascot is a spider.

22 The first pack of hounds was probably imported to southern Maryland in 1650 by Robert Brooks.

23 "Hey! Flim Flam, Bim Bam, Ole Miss, by damn!"

24 Mississippi State University. Black students Jerry Jenkins and Larry Fry were sophomores on the 1972–73 team, which was coached by Kermit Davis.

25 Dean Smith (b. 1931).

26 Paul "Bear" Bryant, Alabama; Eddie Robinson, Grambling; John Heisman, Georgia Tech; Bob Neyland, Tennessee; Frank Howard, Clemson.

27 Walter Lanier Barber (1908–92), known as "Red."

28 Junior Johnson (b. 1931), who in 1963 set what was then an all-time stock car speed record in a one-mile qualifying race of 164.083 mph, then, in the same year, topped that record at 166.005 mph in a five-mile run.

29 Mildred Ella "Babe" Didrikson Zaharias (1914–56).

30 The Pettys: Lee (b. 1914), Richard (b. 1937), and Kyle (b. 1960).

31 Elisha Archie Manning III (b. 1949), today a businessman and sports announcer for the New Orleans Saints. Manning's record still stands.

32 A mile and a quarter.

33 Football.

34 The University of Tennessee–Chattanooga.

35 The Talladega Superspeedway, in Talladega, Alabama – 2.66 miles.

36 Jack Johnson (1878–1946), of whom this song was sung: "Amaze an' Grace, how sweet it sounds / Jack Johnson knocked Jim Jeffries down." Because of his title, Johnson had to flee the South and, eventually, the country.

37 Lee Elder (b. 1934), who entered the Masters in 1975.

38 Jesse Owens (1913–80) and Joe Louis (1914–81).

39 The University of Mississippi. The Dixie National is one of the largest twirling clinics and was the subject of the February 1963 *Esquire* article "Twirling at Ole Miss," by Terry Southern.

40 The Dallas Cowboys and the Houston Oilers.

41 Clemson's. The name was coined in the 1940s by Lonnie McMillian, head coach at Presbyterian College, because he lost so many games in the Clemson stadium. In the mid-1960s, a Clemson graduate presented a white flint rock from Death Valley, California, to Clemson coach Frank Howard. The rock was placed at the top of the east endzone hill. At game time, players enter the stadium here, touch the rock, and then run down the hill, to the delight of around 80,000 screaming fans. *USA Today* has called this tradition "the most exciting twenty-five seconds in college football."

42 University of Maryland Terrapins, University of Virginia Cavaliers, Wake Forest University Demon Deacons, University of North Carolina Tar Heels, North Carolina State University Wolfpack, Duke University Blue Devils, Clemson University Tigers, Georgia Tech Yellow Jackets, and Florida State University Seminoles.

43 Ashel Day, a center for Georgia Tech. He was named All-American in 1918.

44 The Florida Panhandle.

45 Eddie Robinson of Grambling State University.

46 John Heisman, who coached an undefeated Georgia Tech team from 1915 to 1917.

47 A form of poker played by Cajuns in southern Louisiana. In bourré, even penny-ante stakes can suddenly rise to hundreds of dollars on the flash of a single card.

48 Hot Springs, Arkansas. A popular large resort with thermal baths and pools, it was the headquarters of Al Capone and his gang during Prohibition Days.

49 The Evangeline League.

50 Arthur Ashe (1943–93), from Richmond, Virginia, won the U.S. Open in 1968 and Wimbledon in 1975.

51 Ocala, which boasts limestone water, rolling hills, and grassy knolls like those in Kentucky but also has a temperate climate. The area has at least 150 thoroughbred horse farms and has produced several prize-winning horses, including Needles (Kentucky Derby, 1956), Carry Back (Kentucky Derby and Preakness, 1961), and Hail to All (Belmont, 1965).

52 Muhammad Ali, born Cassius Clay. He forfeited the heavyweight title in 1967.

53 Frank McGuire (b. 1916).

54 Level Cross, North Carolina.

55 The Okra Strut, which features a parade, politics, and fried okra.

56 In 1916, the Rambling Wrecks of Georgia Tech scored 222 points against Cumberland University, which scored nothing. Georgia Tech made thirty-two touchdowns.

57 Paul "Bear" Bryant (1913–83).

58 The final practice session before a race.

59 Hilton Head, which is the largest of South Carolina's barrier islands, twelve miles long and covering forty-two square miles.

60 Marion Tinsley, from Humble, Texas, a mathematics professor at Florida State University. He lost only nine games after first winning the world championship.

61 The victory of Centre over Harvard.

62 Frank Howard. He originally hailed from Barlow Bend, Alabama.

63 Florida A&M.

64 Mississippi State. It won the regular season SEC basketball title in 1961, 1962, and 1963.

65 Tony Cloniger, for the Atlanta Braves, on July 3, 1966, against the San Francisco Giants. He had one additional RBI that day, giving him nine for the game, a record for a pitcher.

66 Clemson and Arkansas.

67 Baseball clubs in the Southern Association following World War II: the New Orleans Pelicans, Little Rock Travelers, Memphis Chicks, Nashville Vols, Chattanooga Lookouts, Atlanta Crackers, Birmingham Barons, and the Mobile Bears.

68 Louisiana.

69 Grabbling.

70 Sarah Christian. Although Louise Smith (b. 1916) was the first lady driver and was racing as early as 1945, Christian was the first to compete in a NASCAR-sanctioned race, in 1949. In that race, she qualified twenty-first in a field of forty-four and finished sixth.

71 White Sulphur Springs, Virginia. The Greenbrier, one of the finest resort complexes in the South, was first developed in the late eighteenth century. In 1850, the architect Benjamin Latrobe designed the first of the lovely row cottages. The resort included a ballroom, dining rooms, a bandstand, and a barroom, which was converted to a chapel on Sundays.

72 The University of Georgia. The hedges have now been removed so that the field can be widened to accommodate the 1996 Olympic soccer competition, but clippings have been taken from the plants and will be used to grow a new generation of hedges in time for the next football season.

73 Louisiana State University, where Shaquille O'Neal played before moving on to the pros.

74 The forward pass. The inventor of the forward pass is still a matter of argument, but it was used in a game between the University of North Carolina and the University of Georgia in 1895. The game was witnessed by John Heisman, who was then coaching at Auburn and later recounted the event for *Collier's* magazine.

75 In 1972, Cal Jr. worked as bat boy for the Orioles' Double-A team in Asheville, North Carolina.

76 Dog trials are competitive events where hunting dogs such as beagles, foxhounds, and feists are released into fields and given points by a judge according to their ability to flush out game. While dog trials are not strictly a southern activity, they are often associated with the South because hunting is more prevalent in this region than in others.

77 Arm wrestling. Cleve Dean, from Moultrie, Georgia, retired from competition in 1986 but made a comeback in 1994.

THE LAND

1 The boll weevil, which migrated from Mexico in 1892 and spread terror eastward across the South. It arrived in Louisiana in 1903 and Mississippi in 1907 and spread to the far reaches of the cotton belt by the early 1920s, wreaking havoc on cotton communities and forcing farmers to diversify their crops.

2 The Mississippi River. The largest river in North America, the Mississippi drains a 1,245,000-square-mile area covering all or parts of thirty-one states and two Canadian provinces.

3 Memphis, Tennessee, which lies on the Mississippi River. Memphis was founded in 1819 by land speculators Andrew Jackson, John Overton, and James Winchester on five thousand acres that became available when the Chickasaw Indians were removed.

4 The Natchez Trace, which ends in Natchez, Mississippi. It was cleared as a military road in the early 1800s and today is a scenic and well-traveled road.

5 Salt licks. The trails animals created to these locations were later used by Native Americans and eighteenth-century settlers.

6 Daniel Boone (1734–1820). It ran from Moccasin Gap in southwestern Virginia through the Appalachian Mountains to the Kentucky Bluegrass region.

7 The Tennessee Valley Authority (TVA). By slightly raising or lowering water levels at various dams, the TVA controlled mosquitoes, helping to wipe out a disease that had afflicted one-third of the population.

8 Interstate 495, which encircles Washington, D.C.

9 The blue, the channel, and the flathead, all of the family *Ictaluridae*.

10 Mobile, Alabama, founded in 1702 by French naval officer Jean Baptiste Le Moyne.

11 The red cedar. Cherokees used cedar wood for the litters on which they carried their honored dead.

12 Montgomery, Alabama, founded in 1819 on the site of an Alibamo Indian village named Econchata. The Deep South states selected Montgomery as the site for their secession convention, and Jefferson Davis was inaugurated in the capitol in 1861. In 1955, Montgomery was the scene of the historic bus boycott that initiated the civil disobedience campaigns of the 1950s and 1960s.

13 The Chesapeake Bay.

14 Crisfield, Maryland, which sponsors an annual Miss Crustacean beauty pageant. The Chesapeake Bay yields 50 percent of U.S. blue crab production.

15 The Big Thicket is an area of dense vegetation and wetlands that once covered some three million acres in East Texas and Louisiana. It was named by pioneers entering Texas in the early nineteenth century, who found it difficult to penetrate and detoured around it. About 300,000 acres remain, some of it protected in the Big Thicket National Preserve.

16 Pennsylvania and Maryland. The line was surveyed in 1766.

17 Possum (*Didelphis virginia*).

18 The Blue Ridge Mountains, which stretch from southwestern North Carolina to Gettysburg, Pennsylvania. The haze results from chemicals called terpenes, which are given off by the coniferous trees.

19 Off Cape Hatteras, North Carolina. The area's changing currents, dense fogs, and tricky shoals have led over five hundred ships to founder.

20 Spanish moss, the silver-gray epiphyte that festoons the branches of oaks and other hardwood trees in lowland woodlands from Virginia to Texas.

21 The Tennessee-Tombigbee Waterway, a 234-mile-long manmade inland water route connecting the Gulf of Mexico with the Tennessee River in northeastern Mississippi, linking 16,000 miles of navigable, commercial waterways in at least fourteen states.

22 A devastating flood that inundated 26,000 square miles of land, took 214 lives, drove 637,000 people from their homes, and ruined $236 million worth of property.

23 The cypress, which is relatively resistant to water and can grow in swamps, where its stalagmite-like knees rise above the water and help aerate the tree.

24 Georgia. From the last week of October through May, seven companies around the Cairo, Georgia, area ship 315 tons of collards weekly to the major northeastern metropolitan areas. Half of those collards go to New York City alone.

25 Kudzu, which escaped cultivation and is now categorized as a voracious, annoying weed; it covers some two million acres of forestland. Poet James Dickey has called it the "vegetable form of cancer."

26 The southern magnolia (*Magnolia grandiflora*), sometimes also known as "bull bay."

27 Jekyll Island.

28 Low-level nuclear waste. In the 1960s, the South became the final resting place for much of the radioactive waste generated by the nuclear industry. There are major dump sites at Oak Ridge, Tennessee; Maxey Flats, near Morehead, Kentucky; Savannah River, near Aiken, South Carolina; and Barnwell, South Carolina.

29 Nashville, Tennessee. The Nashville Parthenon was constructed in 1896.

30 Tampa, on the Gulf Coast.

31 False. Measured to the tidewater line, North Carolina has more shoreline on the Atlantic side than Florida does – 3,375 miles, to Florida's 3,331.

32 Louisiana. Parts of New Orleans are eight feet below sea level.

33 Virginia, with 692,000 inhabitants. New York overtook Virginia in the census of 1810.

34 True. The top five are Arizona, Nevada, New Mexico, Oklahoma, and Texas. (But it's not the heat, it's the humidity.)

35 West Virginia. In 1884, the West Virginia tax commission predicted that outside capitalists would "pocket the treasures which lie buried in our hills" and leave the people "poor, helpless, and destitute." This warning proved true: during the twentieth century, the federal government and corporations have exploited Appalachia for its natural resources, mostly timber and coal.

36 Okra (*Hibiscus esculentus*), probably first cultivated in Africa, from whence it got its name: okra is *nkru* in the Ashanti language, and it is also called "gumbo," which comes from the Bantu word *ngombo*.

37 The levees of the Mississippi and its tributaries. These levees stretch over fifteen hundred miles.

38 The Piney Woods, or pine belt of the Southeast, is a region of forestland stretching through nine southern states, from the Carolinas through Georgia and into Texas.

39 The manatee. The current manatee population is probably less than two thousand.

40 The Vieux Carré (pronounced in New Orleans as Voo Car-RAY) is the French Quarter, the original city of New Orleans founded in 1718 by Jean Baptiste Le Moyne, Sieur de Bienville, as a French fortification. The city was ceded to Spain in 1762–63, ceded back to France by Spain, and purchased by the United States in the Louisiana Purchase of 1803.

41 The Carolina parakeet and the passenger pigeon. The Carolina parakeet, North America's only parrot, was aggressive and brightly colored, making it easy prey for hunters and bird catchers since colonial times. The passenger pigeon, too, was overhunted. An early naturalist reported in 1810 that he had seen a flock of migrating pigeons whose numbers he estimated at 2,230,272,000. The last surviving member of each species died in captivity in 1914.

42 The Piedmont. It actually extends from northern Alabama to the Hudson River. At its widest, the Piedmont is 125 miles wide; at its narrowest, a mere ten miles.

43 Spectacular southern gardens.

44 Lake Okeechobee, thirty miles long, thirty miles wide, and fifteen feet deep.

45 The Black Belt.

46 An earthquake, centered near New Madrid, Missouri. It was felt over two-thirds of the United States. Aftershocks continued until February 7, 1812. Another large earthquake occurred near Charleston on August 31, 1886, killing 111 people.

47 A hurricane struck, and three bridges to the mainland were destroyed, preventing evacuation of the city, much of which was less than twenty feet above sea level. It was the worst natural disaster in U.S. history.

48 The larva of the tiger beetle, which one can fish for by inserting a blade of grass into its hole in the ground.

49 Chattanooga. The name really applies to nearby Lookout Mountain.

50 A dragonfly.

51 A system for harvesting mussels in which a long wooden or steel pole with groups of mussel hooks attached is dragged on the river bottom. Musseling is still an important occupation on the rivers of the Upland South.

52 Haiti – then Santo Domingo. During the Haitian Revolution (1791–1803), some fifteen thousand immigrants from Santo Domingo arrived in Louisiana.

53 Mount Mitchell, in the Black Mountains of North Carolina, is 6,684 feet – the highest point east of the Rocky Mountains.

54 The Great Dismal and the Okefenokee. The Dismal Swamp, located on the border of Virginia and North Carolina, covers six hundred square miles; it was originally six times larger, but much of it has been drained for farmland. The Okefenokee Swamp covers seven hundred square miles in southeastern Georgia and parts of Florida.

55 Captain Edward Teach, better known as Blackbeard (?–1718).

56 Natural Bridge, Virginia.

57 Mammoth Cave, Kentucky. Mammoth Cave National Park contains three hundred miles of explored and mapped caves.

58 Hartford, which has a welcome sign to that effect.

59 Picayune, Mississippi, which in 1883 was named for the *New Orleans Daily Picayune*, now the *New Orleans Times-Picayune*. A picayune was a local coin worth around six cents.

60 Natchitoches, Louisiana, founded by the French in 1714, four years before New Orleans.

61 Norfolk, Virginia, home to the U.S. Navy's Atlantic fleet.

62 Jacksonville, at 840 square miles. Juneau, Alaska, is the largest.

63 Hurricane Camille, which first hit land along the Gulf Coast of Mississippi on August 14, 1969, and moved into Virginia through its "back door," or western section. Flash floods killed sixty-seven people in the mountainous regions of the state.

Many bodies were never recovered, and as a result the state legislature declared that persons missing during the storm could be declared dead if they were not found or identified within six months, rather than the usual seven years.

64 The Chesapeake Bay Bridge Tunnel, the world's largest bridge/tunnel complex, is a combination of trestles, bridges, and two tunnels. Built in 1964, the crossing includes tunnels to ensure that the U.S. Navy and commercial ships would have clear channels in and out of the bay even if the bridges were bombed during a war. Before the tunnel was built, travelers were often forced to wait hours for the ferry, which took eighty-five minutes to cross the water.

65 Virginia Beach, Virginia, at Cape Henry. Virginia Beach now claims to be the largest resort city in the world. In 1993 it had thirty-eight miles of shoreline, 259 square miles, and a population of 410,607.

66 Mississippi, Georgia, and Louisiana.

67 Louisiana. The parish system is a vestige of its beginnings under French colonial rule.

68 Hookworm, which thrives in areas without snow cover and in sandy soil, conditions common to the South. Hookworm disease, known as urcinariasis, causes anemia and mental and physical retardation, attributes often associated with rural southerners. In 1911, hookworm infections were reported in 719 out of 884 southern counties. Since World War II, it has been controlled by economic improvement, case treatment, and improved public health and sanitation.

69 The Ozarks.

70 The Federal Road, which began as a mail route in 1806. It was widened to carry troops during the War of 1812 and consequently helped bring settlers into the Deep South from the Upper South. The Federal Road connected with the fall-line cities in Virginia, North Carolina, and South Carolina and continued through Milledgeville, Georgia, and Montgomery and Mobile, Alabama, to New Orleans.

71 The Wiregrass is a region in southeast Alabama and southwest Georgia and includes the cities of Dothan and Enterprise. In the nineteenth century, it was an area of dense pine forests.

sandy, unproductive soil, and expanses of grass thought to be fit only for the pasturage of cattle and hogs. Not until the lumber boom of the late nineteenth century and the rise in the use of fertilizers did people live there in significant numbers.

72 Interstate 285, which forms a loop around the city of Atlanta.

73 A type of pine tree (*Pinus taeda*) found in the central and southeastern United States. This fast-growing tree is often used in reforestation and is a major source of wood for lumber and pulp.

74 Georgia.

75 The coral snake.

76 The River Road.

77 True. In fact, four states – Florida, Texas, Louisiana, and South Carolina – now allow limited gator hunting.

78 Her home was judged to have the nation's worst infestation of cockroaches. Of her dubious honor Lynn says, "We have to shake the shower curtains free from roaches to take a shower. We have to hold our plates at dinner so they won't eat the food and we have to sleep sitting up so roaches won't crawl on us at night."

79 Charlotte, North Carolina, the "Queen City."

80 Tennessee, Maryland, and Virginia – all tobacco-growing states.

81 Mobile, Alabama.

82 Rock City, near Lookout Mountain, Tennessee. Once ubiquitous, the signs are now approaching rarity.

83 Mark Catesby (1679–1749) was the naturalist, and the "chegoe" or chigger is the vicious beast. Catesby was also amazed by his encounters with *Blatta americana*, the cockroach. He reported that roaches were "very troublesome and destructive Vermin, and are so numerous and voracious, that it is impossible to keep victuals of any kind from being devoured by them, without close covering."

84 The Crater of Diamonds State Park, near Murfreesboro, Arkansas, where the general public can search for gems.

85 According to journalist William Ecenbarger, they are U.S. Route 71, near Fayetteville, Arkansas, and Bayou Road in St. Bernard Parish, Louisiana.

HISTORY, POLITICS, AND LAW

1 Nat Turner's Rebellion.

2 Ralph McGill (1898–1969), who held these positions from 1938 until his death.

3 January 15, 1929. In January 1986, eighteen years after his death, King's birthday was declared a national holiday, the first such tribute to a black American.

4 500,000. This move north is often referred to as the Great Migration.

5 Mary Boykin Chesnut (1823–86), whose diaries from February 1861 to July 1865 have been published as *Mary Chesnut's Civil War* (1981).

6 The way west for eastern Indian tribes removed from their lands to make way for white settlers. In the first half of the nineteenth century, the federal government forced one group of Native Americans after another to sign treaties exchanging their homelands for the promise of self-government and new land in what is now Oklahoma. Four of the five "Civilized Tribes" – Cherokees, Chickasaws, Choctaws, and Creeks – were removed on winter marches during which thousands died. Seminoles in Florida resisted removal until 1842, when their leaders were captured.

7 29 percent.

8 Corinne "Lindy" Boggs of Louisiana, whose husband, Hale, went down in an Alaskan plane crash in 1973 and was presumed dead. His body was never found.

9 The Highlander School, established in 1932 by Myles Horton and Don Wes. In 1961, Tennessee confiscated the Monteagle property, and the Highlander School moved to Knoxville, where it continues as the Highlander Research and Education Center and devotes itself to health and environmental issues.

10 "Get down, you damn fool."

11 The Rebel Yell.

12 Nathan Bedford Forrest (1821–77).

13 Formed in 1850, NOSBA was probably the South's first long-shoremen's union.

14 The Grimké sisters, Sarah (1793–1874) and Angelina (1805–79). They arrived in Boston in 1837 and began a lifelong crusade of writing and speaking publicly against slavery.

15 The League of American Wheelmen, the national organization of bicyclists. The Good Roads Movement included the Dixie Highway Association, the Lee Highway Association, and the North and South Bee Line Highway Association.

16 Martha Elizabeth Beall Jennings Mitchell (1918–76), whose blunt and humorous comments on Watergate were both derided and praised. An anonymous floral tribute at her funeral read, "Martha was right."

17 They were all black mayors of major southern cities elected in the 1970s and early 1980s, when African Americans took on greater roles in the politics of the region's cities. Maynard Jackson (elected in 1973) was mayor of Atlanta; Andrew Young (1981), also Atlanta; Richard Arrington (1979), Birmingham; and Ernest "Dutch" Morial (1978), New Orleans.

18 *Brown v. Board of Education of Topeka, Kansas*. The Court's 1955 implementation decree remanded these cases to federal district courts, which were to order desegregation "with all deliberate speed."

19 A bomb blast in the Sixteenth Street Baptist Church, the organizing point for many of the protests in Birmingham, took the lives of four young girls attending Sunday school.

20 Auburn University, which was chartered as the East Alabama Male College in 1856. By 1872, the church did not have enough money to operate the college, so it transferred ownership of the college to the state. The school then became the Agricultural and Mechanical College of Alabama.

21 The Southern Historical Society, founded in 1869 in New Orleans by ex-Confederates dedicated to the vindication of the Lost Cause.

22 Lynching. Between 1882 (when statistics on lynching were first kept) and the early 1950s, a total of almost six thousand people died at the hands of lynch mobs in the United States.

23 Lyndon B. Johnson (1908–73), who hoped that this program would end poverty in the United States.

24 "Paterollers" patrolled plantations, especially at night, to check slave passes, maintain curfews, keep slaves from escaping, and punish those who did.

25 January 21, 1807. In 1889, Georgia became the first state to declare Robert E. Lee's birthday a legal holiday. It is still a state holiday in Alabama, Arkansas, Florida, Georgia, Kentucky, Louisiana, Mississippi, North Carolina, South Carolina, Tennessee, and Virginia. In many of these states, Lee's birthday is combined with Martin Luther King, Jr. Day and celebrated on the third Monday in January. Virginia combines the birthdays of Lee, King, and Andrew Jackson, while Texas celebrates Confederate Heroes Day.

26 Rosa Parks (b. 1913), of Montgomery, Alabama, who refused to give up her bus seat to a white man. Her act inspired African Americans to unite and struggle collectively for change.

27 The Crump machine. Edward H. "Boss" Crump (1874–1954) was mayor in 1909, 1911, and 1915 and remained highly influential in state and local politics until his death in 1954. The Crump machine included the African American community, hence Memphis was one of the few southern cities that allowed blacks to vote, although they were certainly expected to vote for "Mister Crump."

28 The Regulators were vigilantes in the colonial Carolinas in the 1760s and 1770s, who organized to bring responsible government to the backcountry.

29 Ft. Polk, Louisiana, which was considered ideal for training because of environmental conditions similar to those in southeast Asia.

30 Descendants of some of the two thousand Confederate emigrants who went to Brazil after the Civil War. A Fraternity of American Descendants meets quarterly in the cemetery where over four hundred of the ex-Confederates are buried. These Confederate descendants speak Portuguese as well as the southern English dialect of their ancestors.

31 *The Southern Worker*. The Communist Party expanded its activities in the South during the Great Depression.

32 Henry W. Grady (1850–89). A journalist, and part owner and managing editor of the *Atlanta Constitution*, Grady energetically campaigned for a New South – a region that would, through industrialization, rise phoenixlike from the ashes of the Civil War.

33 Key West, Florida.

34 Jessie Daniel Ames (1883–1972) of Texas. Nine years later the organization had 40,000 members. In 1943 it was absorbed by the Southern Regional Council.

35 Frederick Augustus Porter Barnard (1809–89), for whom Barnard College, the sister college of Columbia University, was named.

36 Marian Wright Edelman (b. 1939). An attorney, Edelman was named one of the "four most exciting young women in America" by *Mademoiselle* in 1965, an "Outstanding Young Woman" by *Vogue* for 1965–66, and one of the "100 Most Influential Women in America" by *Ladies' Home Journal* in 1983. In 1985 she received a MacArthur Foundation award for her work for children and civil rights.

37 The Ku Klux Klan, founded in 1866 at Pulaski, Tennessee, by six former Confederates.

38 Birmingham. News photos of protesting blacks being attacked by snarling police dogs spread that image of the city worldwide.

39 Button Gwinnett, of Georgia. Gwinnett died in a duel in the following year, leaving few examples of his signature.

40 Gastonia.

41 True. Both were born in Kentucky to yeoman farming parents, within one hundred miles of each other and separated by only a few months. The Davises moved South to Mississippi and made a fortune in cotton. Lincoln's family moved to Illinois and a quite different destiny.

42 Ti-Grace Atkinson (b. 1939), whose southern background and elegant, "ladylike" appearance softened the "man-eating" image of the National Organization of Women, from which she later resigned. In 1974, she published a collection of her speeches and writings entitled *Amazon Odyssey*.

43 Lord Cornwallis surrendered to General George Washington there on October 19, 1781, marking the end of the American Revolution.

44 General Andrew Jackson (1767–1845), of South Carolina and Tennessee, whose troops defeated the British at the Battle of New Orleans in 1812.

45 Comer. Woodward (b. 1908) was born in Vanndale, Arkansas, and is currently Sterling Professor of History Emeritus at Yale University.

46 Theodore Bilbo, Mississippi; Tom Watson, Georgia; Ben Tillman, South Carolina; Huey Long, Louisiana; George Wallace, Alabama.

47 Slavery. While the institution was fading away in the Western world in the nineteenth century, it became an essential part of the aristocratic Old South. Even the masses of southern whites who owned no slaves supported slavery as a means of keeping blacks subordinate.

48 Granny.

49 Little Rock, Arkansas, to enforce court-ordered school desegregation.

50 In 1861, the Chickasaw tribe joined the Confederacy and fought in several campaigns against Union troops in the Indian territory (Oklahoma).

51 General Andrew Jackson (1767–1845), whose "Hunters of Kentucky" had a larger-than-life reputation as sharpshooting, wily frontiersmen.

52 George Corley Wallace (b. 1919), who unsuccessfully tried to prevent integration at the University of Alabama.

53 All were civil rights organizations: the National Association for the Advancement of Colored People, the Southern Christian Leadership Conference, the Congress of Racial Equality, and the Student Non-violent Coordinating Committee.

54 South Carolina, which seceded on December 20, 1860. South Carolina was followed, in order, by Mississippi, Florida, Alabama, Georgia, Louisiana, Texas, Virginia, Arkansas, Tennessee, and North Carolina.

55 The Southern Tenant Farmers' Union, which attempted to bring small farm owners together with tenants and farm laborers of both races and sexes.

56 Harlan County, known as "Bloody Harlan." During the coal mine strife of the 1930s, eleven struggle-related deaths and twenty woundings were recorded there.

57 In South Carolina, Union troops tore rails from railroad beds, heated them, and twisted them around trees.

58 The Oil Workers International in Ft. Worth, Texas. Its Texas-Louisiana district became the largest branch of the union and took the lead in the 1945 nationwide strike that established oil workers as the highest-paid manufacturing hands in the country.

59 The Charles Town (Charleston) Library Society, founded in 1773.

60 James Meredith (b. 1933). This event resulted in rioting and two deaths.

61 W. W. Williams, born in Itawamba County, Mississippi, died in Houston, Texas, on December 20, 1959, at the ripe old age of 117 years. He claimed that he joined the Confederate army at the age of twenty-two and served as forage master for Hood's Brigade. War records in the National Archives do not list Mr. Williams as a member of the Confederate army, and there was some controversy over whether or not he had actually served in the war. But an Act of Congress, signed by President Eisenhower in 1959, proclaimed the day of Williams's death a day of national mourning. As the president observed, "With Mr. Williams' passing, the hosts of blue and gray who were the chief actors in that great and tragic drama a century ago have all passed from the world stage. No longer are they the blue and gray. All rest together as Americans in honor and glory. An era has ended" (*New York Times*, December 21, 1959). Incidentally, although the South lost the war, its soldiers outlived those of the North. The last Union army veteran died in 1956.

62 The Salzburgers, who were first evicted from Germany on October 31, 1731, under the Edict of Expulsion, which required them to leave the country within eight days.

63 Approximately 35.7 percent, according to 1980 figures.

64 Jimmy Carter (b. 1924), of Plains, Georgia.

65 The "Southern Manifesto," a response to the *Brown v. Board of Education* decision. The signers pledged to "use all lawful means to bring about a reversal of this decision which is contrary to the Constitution and to prevent the use of force in its implementation."

66 Theodore Bilbo (1877–1947), who first entered politics in 1903 but was defeated for county clerk by a one-armed Confederate veteran whom Bilbo said he might vote for himself. He was elected governor of Mississippi in 1915 and 1927 and was elected U.S. senator in 1934, 1940, and 1946.

67 "Dixiecrats," a term coined by Bill Weisner of the *Charlotte News and Observer*.

68 Orval Eugene Faubus (1910–95), originally from the Ozark community of Combs.

69 James Elisha "Big Jim" Folsom (b. 1908), of Coffee County, Alabama, who won the governorship in 1946 and 1954. He was defeated in 1962 by George Wallace.

70 Rebecca Ann Latimer Felton (1835–1930), a complicated figure who was a temperance supporter, a suffragette, a writer, and, as should be obvious, an outspoken cultural commentator.

71 Jacob Thompson, of Oxford, Mississippi. Thompson was President Buchanan's secretary of the interior.

72 Lester Maddox (b. 1915). Georgia's citizens elected him governor in January 1967.

73 Claude Pepper (1900–1989). Born on his family's farm near Dudleyville, Alabama, Pepper was one of Florida's senators from 1936 to 1950, when he was defeated by George Smathers in a campaign notable for the vitriolic smears launched against him. Pepper has said, "I refuse to believe that a country as rich and powerful as ours can't afford to guarantee the basic comfort and security of its older citizens. I know we can do it, and I intend to be long and loud about it."

74 West Virginia, which abolished capital punishment in 1965.

75 Hernando de Soto, who on his 1541 expedition became the first European to see the Mississippi River. He became ill after crossing the river, and his body was buried in the river near present-day Ferriday, Louisiana.

76 Sharecroppers. The sharecropper class included the parents of writers Richard Wright, Alice Walker, and Harry Crews.

77 Judah P. Benjamin (1811–84), one of the ten thousand southern Jews who served in the Confederacy.

78 Lillian Jackson Carter (1898–1983), daughter of a Richland, Georgia, postmaster and mother of Jimmy Carter, the thirty-ninth president.

79 The towns of Rohwer and Jerome, Arkansas, where nearly 16,000 Japanese Americans from the West Coast were interned between 1942 and 1945.

80 Davy Crockett (1786–1836), who was born in Greene County, Tennessee, and died at the Alamo.

81 "Light Horse Harry" Lee (1756–1818). The elder Lee was born in Dumfries, Virginia. A Revolutionary War hero, he participated in the battles of Brandywine, Germantown, and Monmouth. His most famous exploit was the capture of the British post in Paulus Nook, New Jersey. The nickname stemmed from his highly mobile maneuvers in the American cavalry.

82 Thad Cochran and Trent Lott, Republicans from Mississippi. They both attended Ole Miss.

83 Alvin C. York (1887–1964), of Pall Mall, Tennessee. The 1941 film based on his life, *Sergeant York*, starred Gary Cooper.

84 Adolph Ochs (1858–1935).

85 The *Sultana*. The explosion occurred a short distance above Memphis, Tennessee, and killed 1,450 Union soldiers who were on their way home from the war.

86 Preston Brooks (1819–75). Sumner had given a speech criticizing the South and, in particular, Brooks's old relative Andrew Butler, whom Sumner said had a habit of expectorating when he spoke. Brooks was infuriated and beat Sumner with a gutta-percha cane.

87 General Pierre Gustave Toutant de Beauregard (1818–93).

88 Civil rights activist Fannie Lou Hamer (1917–77), of Ruleville, Mississippi, one of the founders of the Mississippi Freedom Democratic Party.

89 The Julius Rosenwald Fund.

90 Denmark Vesey, a free black who, along with his thirty-four slave accomplices, was tried, convicted, and executed for an alleged plot to murder the white population of Charleston and set fire to the city. The Citadel was established in response to the uprising to "insure domestic tranquility."

91 Mississippi, which today is the only southern state to permit conjugal visits.

92 "Fighting Joe" Wheeler (1836–1906) and Fitzhugh Lee (1835–1905), nephew of Robert E. Lee. During the Spaniards' retreat, Wheeler was heard to yell, "We've got the damn Yankees on the run."

93 Charleston, South Carolina.

94 Kitty Hawk, N.C. Orville and Wilbur Wright of Dayton, Ohio, chose a hundred-foot-high sand dune there as the site for their first successful airplane flight in 1903. The Wright Brothers' National Memorial was created there in 1927.

95 Georgia, which abolished them in 1940. In 1995, Alabama reinstituted them.

96 Jimmy Carter (b. 1924). In a November 1976 interview, Carter said, "I've looked on a lot of women with lust. I've committed adultery in my heart many times. This is something that God recognizes I will do, and God forgives me for it."

97 James Madison (1751–1836), who was elected fourth president of the United States in 1809. His resolutions were aimed at the Alien and Sedition Acts, which he charged were unconstitutional, but he was later embarrassed when they were employed by states'-righters in the nullification controversy.

98 Barbara Jordan (b. 1936) of Texas, and Andrew Young (b. 1932) of Georgia. In 1994, Jordan won the Medal of Freedom.

99 Strom Thurmond (b. 1902). Ralph Yarborough of Texas was the unfortunate senator who was pinned in this incident. Thurmond could also be a poster-boy for May-December marriages: he married his wife Nancy in 1969, when he was sixty-six and she was twenty-two. The couple separated in 1991 after twenty-two years of marriage and four children.

100 Tobacco. King James I, however, opposed the habit: he called tobacco a "stinking weed" and smoking "a custome Lothsome to the eye, hatefull to the Nose, harmfull to the braine, dangerous to the lungs."

101 Eugene Talmadge (1884–1946). With his demagogic "populist agrarianist" style, he drew crowds of 20,000 to 30,000 folks to rallies that included barbecue, corn liquor, and country music.

102 Eliza Lucas Pinckney (1723–93), an educated and industrious woman who managed three family indigo plantations.

103 Three. There were three regulation issues of underwear each year. Actual issues were, of course, subject to availability.

104 Patrick Henry (1736–99), one of the greatest orators in American history, whose "Give me liberty or give me death" speech on March 23, 1775, in St. John's Church in Richmond made him the South's first rebel.

105 Marcus Dupree (b. 1964), who later played for the Portland Breakers.

106 *The Emancipator*, first published in 1820 in Jonesborough, Tennessee, by Elihu Embree.

107 "Commodore" Cornelius Vanderbilt (1794–1877), who gave money for the endowment of Nashville's Vanderbilt University in 1873.

108 Virginian Thomas Jefferson (1743–1826).

109 The first Dutch ships arrived at Jamestown in 1619.

110 Tom Watson (1856–1922) of Thomson, Georgia, whose family lost its valuable plantation after the Civil War. Watson did not cotton to the New South call for industrialization; he believed instead that the South should become a region of prosperous farmers through reformation of the prevailing economy.

111 Captain Henry Wirz, commander of the inner stockade at Andersonville prison, on the charge of cruelty. Witnesses later testified that he was not personally responsible for events at the prison, and he was exonerated.

112 Georgia. Gold was discovered at Dahlonega in 1829, on land owned until that time by the Cherokee Indians.

113 Warm Springs, Georgia. Roosevelt died there in 1945.

114 April 9, 1865, at Appomattox Court House, Virginia.

115 The College of William and Mary, founded in 1693 in Williamsburg, Virginia. Harvard, founded in 1636, was first.

116 Cordell Hull (1871–1955), whom President Truman called the "Father of the United Nations." Hull's Cumberland Mountain roots instilled in him a strong and unwavering sense of right and wrong – "mountain justice," which served the United States well during World War II.

117 Georgia, Florida, Arkansas, Alabama, and Mississippi.

118 Andrew Young (b. 1932), who was appointed by Jimmy Carter.

119 The *H. L. Hunley*, built by the Confederates, had no engine and was propeller-driven by an eight-man crew. Carried from Mobile and reassembled at Charleston Harbor, the *Hunley* proved unsuccessful: the crews in three trial dives were killed. Horrified by the ghastly spectacle of his drowned men, General Beauregard banned the underwater use of the vessel. In 1864, the *Hunley* rammed the Union sloop *Housatonic*, sending both vessels to the bottom of the sea. The remains of the Confederate sub were discovered just off the coast of South Carolina in May 1995.

120 Louisiana State Seminary of Learning, now Louisiana State University.

121 The Equal Rights Amendment.

122 Mississippi and Georgia.

123 *Plessy v. Ferguson* (1896). In the train incident that provoked the case, Homer Adolph Plessy was trying to get from New Orleans to Covington, Louisiana, and refused to leave the all-white car.

124 William Jennings Bryan (1860–1925).

125 Texas A&M.

126 Montgomery, Alabama.

127 Sam Ervin (1896–1985), a conservative Democrat, who headed the Senate committee investigating the Watergate affair and fought President Nixon's effort to withhold evidence and testimony on the ground of executive privilege.

128 Helen Keller (1880–1968), of Tuscumbia, Alabama.

129 At Roanoke Island, in what is now North Carolina. The island was settled in 1586 under the direction of Sir Walter Raleigh. By 1590, the entire colony had disappeared, under circumstances that still remain a mystery.

130 Andrew Jackson (N.C., 1767–1845, seventh); William Henry Harrison (Va., 1773–1841, ninth); John Tyler (Va., 1790–1862, tenth); James K. Polk (N.C., 1795–1849, eleventh); Zachary Taylor (Va., 1784–1850, twelfth); Abraham Lincoln (Ky., 1809–65, sixteenth); Andrew Johnson (N.C., 1808–75, seventeenth); Woodrow Wilson (Va., 1856–1924, twenty-eighth); Jimmy Carter (Ga., b. 1924, thirty-ninth); and Bill Clinton (Ark., b. 1946, forty-second).

131 Daniel Boone (1734–1820), who is best known for his pioneer spirit and exploration and settlement of the southern frontier. Dan Beard, founder of the Boy Scouts of America, based his conception of the organization on the following premise: "A society of scouts to be identified with the greatest of all scouts, Daniel Boone, and to be known as the Sons of Daniel Boone."

132 Booker T. Washington (1856–1915), born a slave in Franklin County, Virginia. Washington became one of the foremost black educators of the nineteenth and early twentieth centuries.

133 Fayette, Mississippi.

134 Wilbur Mills (1909–92), an Arkansas representative, was chairman of the House Ways and Means Committee in the 1970s. One night in 1974, Mills was stopped for speeding near the Jefferson Memorial in Washington. He was drunk, and his date, stripper Fanne Foxe, got out and leaped into the Tidal Basin. Mills and Foxe kept up an affair, and the House was finally forced to take away Mills's chairmanship.

135 On January 1, 1863, President Lincoln issued the Emancipation Proclamation, which abolished slavery in the states in rebellion. The Thirteenth Amendment, which became law in December 1865, prohibited slavery in the rest of the country.

136 Osceola (1800–1838).

137 The madness for land that occurred after the removal of Native Americans in 1814. Settlers from the Upper South began moving into Alabama at an unprecedented pace, trying to obtain some of the rich lands in the newly organized state. Population figures for the state attest to the rise: in 1800, there were 1,250 residents; in 1810, there were 9,046; in 1820, 127,901; and in 1830, 309,525.

138 L. Douglas Wilder (b. 1931), who was elected governor of Virginia in 1990. In 1969, he became the first African American state senator in Virginia since Reconstruction.

139 St. Augustine, Florida, settled in 1565 by Don Pedro Menendez de Aviles.

140 James William Fulbright (1905–95).

141 Doc Holliday (1852–87), whose given name was John Henry Holliday.

142 Historically, a southern white who was so committed to voting for the Democratic Party, as the whites-only party, that he or she would even vote for a mongrel yellow dog if it ran for office as a Democrat.

143 On April 10, 1993, Guy Hunt was forced to resign, as required by law, after being convicted of diverting money from an inaugural fund for his own personal use. Lieutenant Governor Jim Folsom Jr. immediately took office.

144 Pensacola, Florida.

145 Earl Warren (1891–1974), chief justice of the Supreme Court from 1953 to 1969, handed down the court's unanimous *Brown v. Board of Education* decision and several other controversial cases. He upheld the 1964 Civil Rights Act, found miscegenation laws unconstitutional, and prohibited prayer in schools. Denunciations of the court's rulings often turned into personal attacks on Warren.

146 24 percent. An estimated 26,000 to 31,000 Confederates died in federal prisons. Approximately 13,000 federal soldiers died at Andersonville.

147 Black Monday.

148 He was assassinated in 1863 by a Dr. Peters of Spring Hill, Tennessee, who suspected him (probably correctly) of philandering with the good doctor's young wife. Later, Peters was acquitted, remarried his wife, moved to Arkansas, and was elected to the state legislature.

149 The Orangeburg Massacre.

150 "They couldn't hit an elephant at this range."

151 Approximately 35 percent.

152 Sequoyah, born near Fort Loudon on the Tennessee River around 1760. His wife burned his work, but he started over, finally perfecting a Cherokee syllabary in 1821. He died in 1843.

153 Jones County, in southeastern Mississippi, was strongly anti-Confederate and, according to legend, seceded from the state late in 1862, creating an independent republic with its own legislature and president. In fact, it was a haven for deserters and alienated Union soldiers.

154 Huey Pierce Long (1893–1935), the legendary governor and senator from Louisiana, who liked to refer to himself as the Kingfish. In 1933, as senator, he proposed his Share Our Wealth program, which was to be a massive plan of tax reform to redistribute the nation's wealth. Although there was always corruption and controversy surrounding Long, he was a man of many talents, as his song "Every Man a King," written with Castro Carazo and recorded by Newman on *Good Old Boys*, attests.

155 Newt Gingrich (b. 1946), speaker of the House, who is really from Pennsylvania. The first statement was quoted in *Esquire*, October 1989; the second was quoted in the *Atlantic*, June 1993.

156 Hilton Head Island, South Carolina, where Mitchelville was created in 1862. The village, which is near the modern-day airport, was named for General Ormsby M. Mitchel. It elected its own mayor and council and established one of the first compulsory education systems in the South.

157 Savannah, Georgia, which fell in December 1864.

158 Not Captain John Smith, whom she befriended and helped to establish relations with her tribe when she was about ten years old, but John Rolfe, a tobacco planter whom she married on April 5, 1614, in Jamestown. In 1616, Pocahontas, Rolfe, their son Thomas, and a group of over ten Powhatan Indians traveled to England, where they were received enthusiastically by the King, the royal family, and the court. Just as the group was scheduled to leave, Pocahontas became ill and died. She is buried at St. George's Church in Gravesend, England. Pocahontas and Rolfe's descendants include members of the Randolph, Blair, Bolling, and Lewis families. The Pepper Bird Foundation, an organization devoted to the preservation of Native American heritage in Virginia, complains that in the Walt Disney film version of Pocahontas's story, "historical fact was thrown out the window. . . . The beautiful message of American history is lost, but is the one to keep in your heart."